Name _____

| September | Year _____ | Season |
| --- | --- | --- |
| | | winter    summer<br>spring    autumn |

Parents, please post this calendar. Help your children with the items below.

| Sunday | Monday | Tuesday | Wednesday | Thursday | Friday | Saturday |
| --- | --- | --- | --- | --- | --- | --- |
| | | | | | | |
| | | | | | | |
| | | | | | | |
| | | | | | | |
| | | | | | | |

1. Write the number for each day in September.

2. There are always _____ days in September.

3. There are _____ Mondays in September this year.

4. Color the first day of school red.

5. Draw a leaf on the first day of autumn.

6. Record class birthdays on your calendar.

Seasonal Activities • EMC 2003 • © Evan-Moor Corp.

Name _____.

# October

| Year | Season |
|------|--------|
| _____ | winter    summer<br>spring    autumn |

Parents, please post this calendar. Help your children with the items below.

| Sunday | Monday | Tuesday | Wednesday | Thursday | Friday | Saturday |
|--------|--------|---------|-----------|----------|--------|----------|
|        |        |         |           |          |        |          |
|        |        |         |           |          |        |          |
|        |        |         |           |          |        |          |
|        |        |         |           |          |        |          |
|        |        |         |           |          |        |          |

1. Write the number for each day in October.

2. There are always _____ days in October.

3. Circle the days of the week you go to school.

4. Draw a boat on Columbus Day.

5. Draw a black cat on Halloween.

6. Record class birthdays on your calendar.

Name _____

| | Year | Season |
|---|---|---|
| **November** | _____ | winter summer<br>spring autumn |

Parents, please post this calendar. Help your children with the items below.

| Sunday | Monday | Tuesday | Wednesday | Thursday | Friday | Saturday |
|---|---|---|---|---|---|---|
| | | | | | | |
| | | | | | | |
| | | | | | | |
| | | | | | | |
| | | | | | | |

1. Write the number for each day in November.

2. There are always _____ days in November.

3. Name the first day of the week. _____

4. Name the last day of the week. _____

5. Draw a Pilgrim's hat on Thanksgiving Day.

6. Record class birthdays on your calendar.

Seasonal Activities • EMC 2003 • © Evan-Moor Corp.

Name _____

# Back to School

Color the tools you use at school. Check them off the list below.

_____ book              _____ crayon            _____ scissors
_____ pencil            _____ ruler             _____ paintbrush

## What else is hiding in this picture?

_____

Name _____

# A Busy Day at School

Draw. Write.

| This is my teacher. | This is me. |

My teacher's name is

_____ .

My teacher _____

_____

_____ at school.

I am in _____ grade.

I _____

_____

at school.

# What Is It?

Start at **1**. Connect the dots.

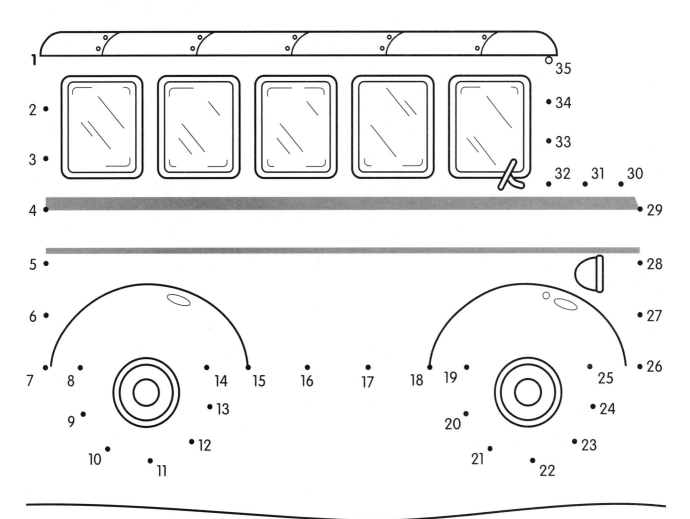

1
2 •
3 •
4 •
5 •
6 •
7  8
9
10  11  12  13  14  15  16  17  18  19  20  21  22  23  24  25  26  27  28  29  30  31  32  33  34  35

Circle the way you get to school.

Name _____

# At School

Fill in the boxes to name the pictures.

Seasonal Activities • EMC 2003 • © Evan-Moor Corp.

Name _____

# School Word Search

Find the words in the puzzle.

| b | o | o | k | d | r | a | w | s |
|---|---|---|---|---|---|---|---|---|
| l | u | n | c | h | x | g | r | c |
| b | m | p | a | p | e | r | e | h |
| u | a | p | p | l | e | s | a | o |
| s | p | e | n | c | i | l | d | o |
| t | e | a | c | h | e | r | x | l |

**Word Box**

| ✔ book | ___ lunch | ___ read |
|--------|-----------|----------|
| ___ bus | ___ paper | ___ school |
| ___ draw | ___ pencil | ___ teacher |

Fill in the missing word.

1. I like to _____ frogs with my green crayon.

2. My teacher likes to _____ to the class.

3. May I sharpen my _____?

4. I rode the _____ to _____ today.

# School Rhymes

Find the word that rhymes. Write it on the line.

| | | |
|---|---|---|
| book<br>_look_ | school<br>_____ | play<br>_____ |
| table<br>_____ | lunch<br>_____ | bus<br>_____ |
| draw<br>_____ | teach<br>_____ | flag<br>_____ |
| class<br>_____ | clock<br>_____ | read<br>_____ |

**Word Box**

| | | | |
|---|---|---|---|
| ___ able | ___ bunch | ✔ look | ___ stay |
| ___ bag | ___ glass | ___ reach | ___ tool |
| ___ bead | ___ lock | ___ saw | ___ us |

# Autumn Weather

Color the picture.

Fill in the blanks.

_____ is the first day of autumn.
date

## The weather is _____ .

Name _____

# Acorn Hunt

Cut out the puzzle. Glue the pieces in order in the frame.
Circle the acorns.

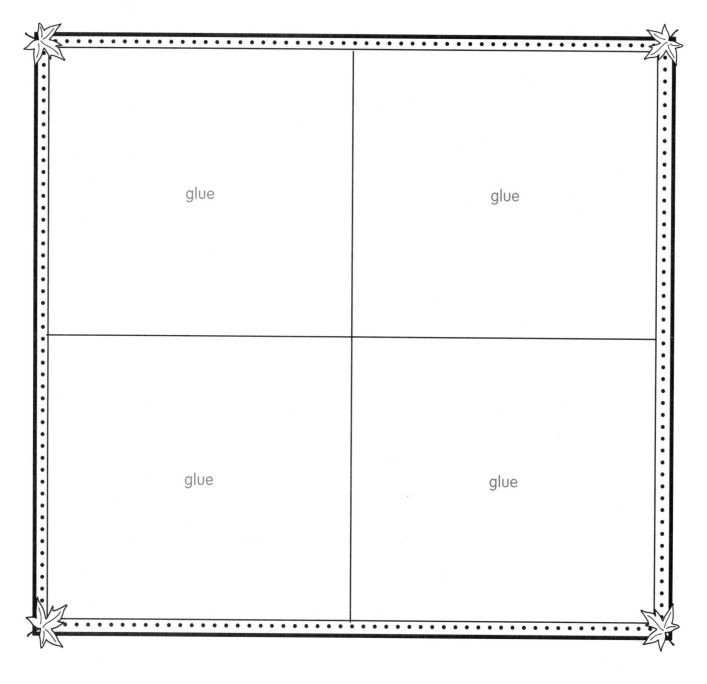

How many acorns did you find? ☐

**Note:** Reproduce this puzzle to use with the frame on page 12.

Name _____

# Leaves Change Color

Color the leaves on the trees.

_____ **Summer** _____

**I**n summer, the leaves on the trees are green.

_____ **Autumn** _____

**I**n autumn, the leaves on some trees change color. The leaves turn red, yellow, and orange.

The leaves fall off the trees.

Seasonal Activities • EMC 2003 • © Evan-Moor Corp.

Name _____

# Falling Leaves

Find the words.
Circle them.

o z (b r o w n) r y
r v h l b h m a e
a t b f a l l k l
n w i n d y b e l
g t r e e r e d o
e q c l e a f u w

**Word Box**

✓ brown ___ red
___ fall ___ tree
___ leaf ___ windy
___ orange ___ yellow

Write a sentence about autumn leaves.

_____

_____ .

Name _____

# Gathering Nuts

In the autumn, squirrels are very busy.
They must find food to save for winter.

How many nuts has the squirrel picked up? Add the nuts together to see.

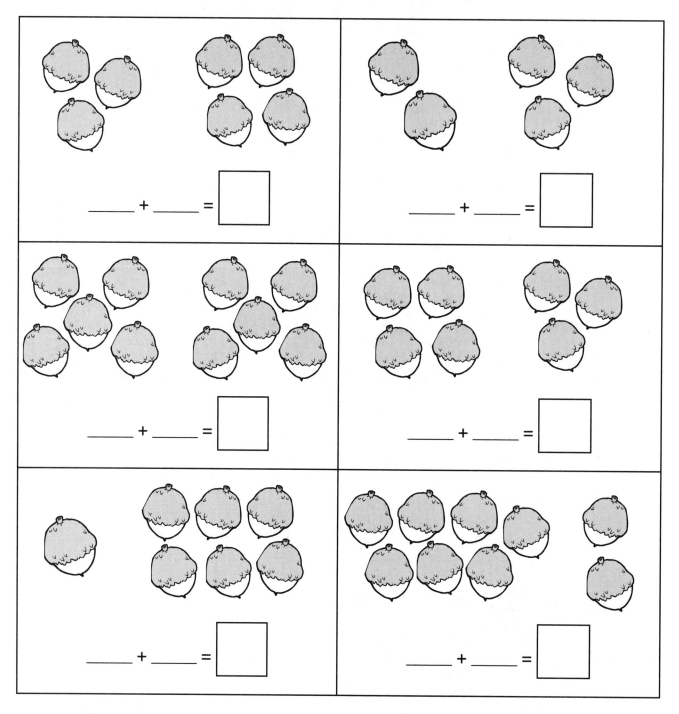

_____ + _____ = ☐

_____ + _____ = ☐

_____ + _____ = ☐

_____ + _____ = ☐

_____ + _____ = ☐

_____ + _____ = ☐

Seasonal Activities • EMC 2003 • © Evan-Moor Corp.

Name _____

# What Goes Together?

Find the words that
go together.
Write them on the lines.

| | | |
|---|---|---|
| tree <br> __leaf__ | sock <br> _____ | hot dog <br> _____ |
| mitten <br> _____ | hammer <br> _____ | bat <br> _____ |
| hat <br> _____ | bee <br> _____ | nest <br> _____ |

**Word Box**

| ___ ball | ___ hand | ✔ leaf |
|---|---|---|
| ___ bird | ___ head | ___ nail |
| ___ bun | ___ honey | ___ shoe |

Name _____

# Autumn Crossword Puzzle

Fill in the boxes.

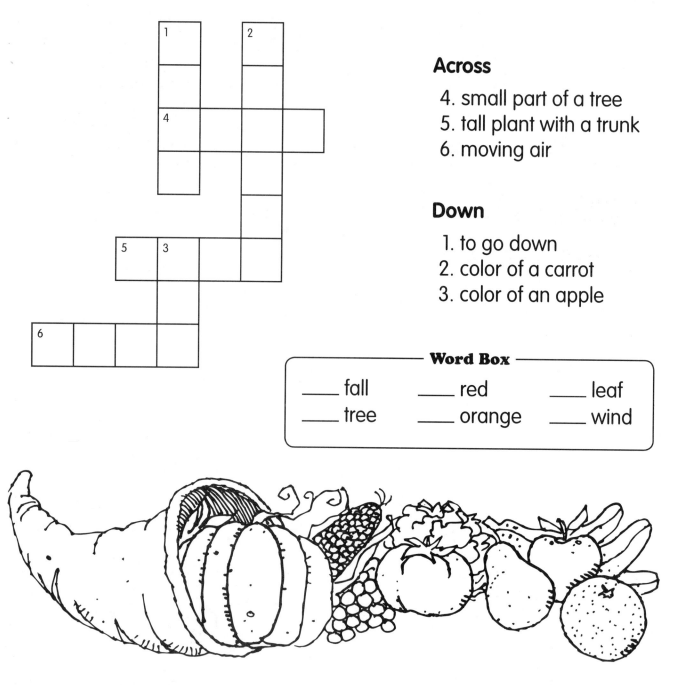

## Across

4. small part of a tree
5. tall plant with a trunk
6. moving air

## Down

1. to go down
2. color of a carrot
3. color of an apple

**Word Box**

____ fall      ____ red      ____ leaf
____ tree     ____ orange   ____ wind

Color the picture above.

Which one do you like best? _____

Seasonal Activities • EMC 2003 • © Evan-Moor Corp.

# Christopher Columbus

Cut on the lines. Put the pages in order. Staple the pages together. Color.

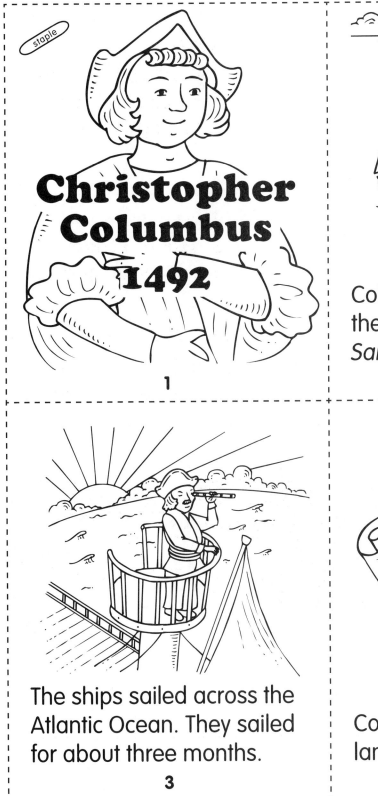

staple

**Christopher Columbus 1492**

1

Columbus had three ships: the *Nina*, the *Pinta*, and the *Santa Maria*.

2

The ships sailed across the Atlantic Ocean. They sailed for about three months.

3

Columbus found the land we call America.

4

Name _____

# Across the Ocean

Help Columbus find America by coloring the numbers used to count by **2s**.

| 1 | 0 | 2 | 4 | 3 | 5 |
|---|---|---|---|---|---|
| 17 | 10 | 9 | 6 | 8 | 7 |
| 16 | 2 | 12 | 11 | 10 | 12 |
| 4 | 15 | 13 | 18 | 16 | 14 |
| 5 | 6 | 14 | 20 | 7 | 8 |

Count by **2s**.

0, _____, _____, _____, _____, _____,

_____, _____, _____, _____, _____,

Seasonal Activities • EMC 2003 • © Evan-Moor Corp.

Name _____

# Magic Vine

Color the pictures.

A fairy seed I planted,
So dry and white and old.
There sprang a vine enchanted
With magic flowers of gold.

I watched it, I tended it,
And truly, by and by,
It bore a jack-o'-lantern,
And a great Thanksgiving pie.

*Unknown*

Name _____

# Watch the Pumpkin Grow

Color and cut out the pictures. Glue them in order.

| 1 | 2 | 3 |
|---|---|---|
| glue | glue | glue |

| 4 | 5 | 6 |
|---|---|---|
| glue | glue | glue |

I pick the big pumpkin.

See the plant grow.

Little pumpkins start to grow.

Flowers grow on the vine.

I plant the seed.

Now I have a jack-o'-lantern.

Name _____

# Green and Orange Surprise

Start at **1**. Connect the dots.
Color the picture.

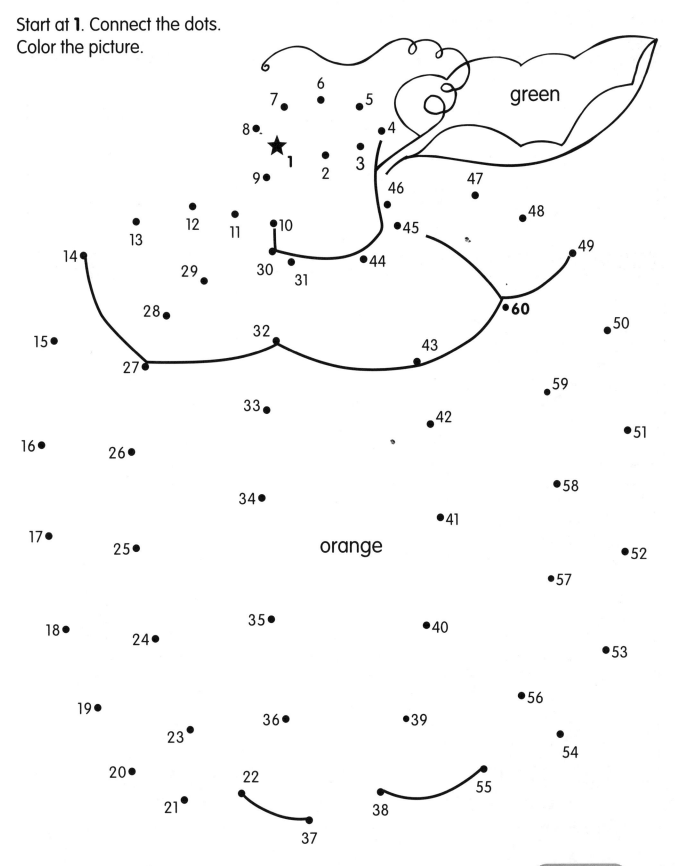

Name _____

# Scarecrow

Draw the other side. Color the picture.

Scarecrow stands in the field all day,
waving his arms to scare birds away.

Seasonal Activities • EMC 2003 • © Evan-Moor Corp.

Name _____

# Halloween Word Search

Find the words.

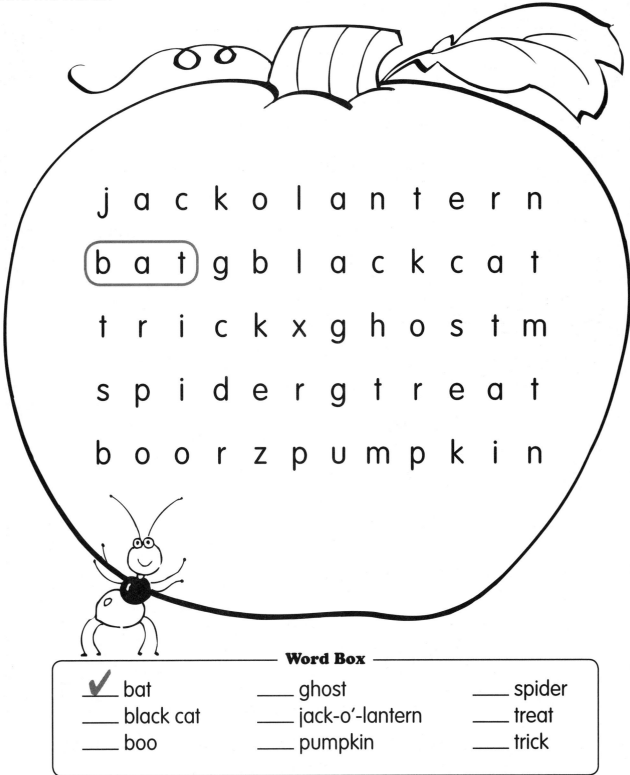

```
j  a  c  k  o  l  a  n  t  e  r  n
b  a  t  g  b  l  a  c  k  c  a  t
t  r  i  c  k  x  g  h  o  s  t  m
s  p  i  d  e  r  g  t  r  e  a  t
b  o  o  r  z  p  u  m  p  k  i  n
```

## Word Box

✔ bat          ___ ghost              ___ spider
___ black cat  ___ jack-o'-lantern    ___ treat
___ boo        ___ pumpkin            ___ trick

Name _____

# Mystery Words

Unscramble the words.
Draw lines to match the words to the pictures.

1. tab

___ ___ ___

2. wol

___ ___ ___

3. hstgo

___ ___ ___ ___ ___

4. thiwc

___ ___ ___ ___ ___

5. munpipk

___ ___ ___ ___ ___ ___ ___

6. bklca atc

___ ___ ___ ___ ___   ___ ___ ___

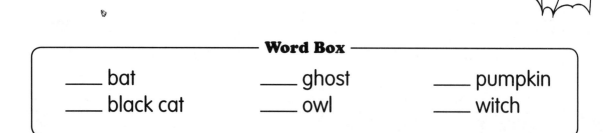

**Word Box**

| ___ bat | ___ ghost | ___ pumpkin |
| ___ black cat | ___ owl | ___ witch |

26  **Autumn**                    Seasonal Activities • EMC 2003 • © Evan-Moor Corp.

Name _____

# A Black Cat

Follow the directions to draw a cat.

Color the cat black. Add a big yellow moon.

# The Mayflower Story

Cut on the lines. Put the pages in order. Staple them together.

staple

**The Mayflower**

On September 6, 1620, the *Mayflower* set sail from England.

1

The Pilgrims were on the *Mayflower*. It was very crowded on the boat.

2

They sailed across the Atlantic Ocean. They were going to America. They sailed for many weeks.

3

They landed at Plymouth. They started a new life in a new land.

4

Name _____

# The Mayflower

Start at **1**. Connect the dots.

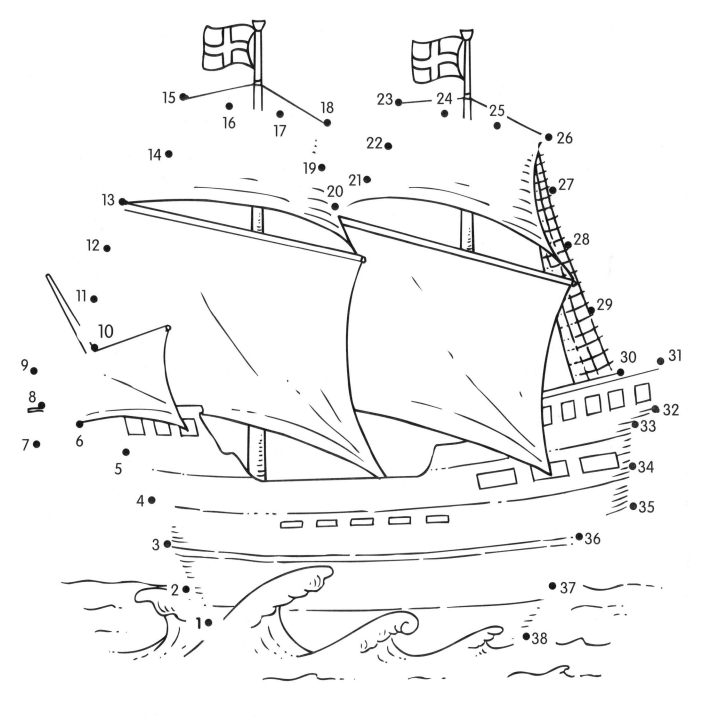

Who sailed on the *Mayflower?* _____

_____

# The Pilgrims

Cut on the lines.
Put the pages in order.
Staple the pages together.

If You Were a Pilgrim

You might live in
this kind of house.

---

staple

# If You Were a Pilgrim

You might live in
this kind of house.

1

You might wear
these clothes.

2

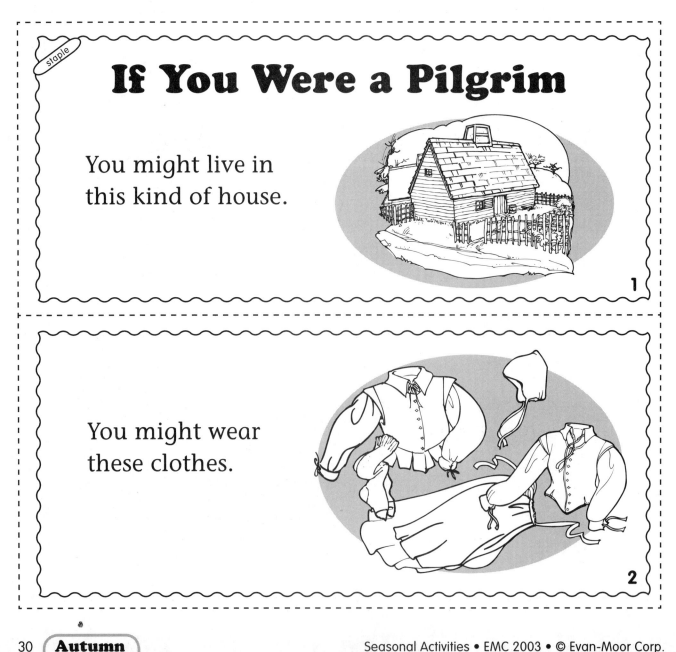

You might use
these tools.

**3**

You might read
this kind of
schoolbook.

**4**

You might eat
these kinds
of food.

**5**

# Squanto

Color the picture.

**S**quanto was a Native American.

He helped the Pilgrims.

He showed them how to plant corn, pumpkins, and beans.

He showed them how to find clams and eels.

He showed them how to find wild berries.

He showed them how to hunt for deer, bears, and turkeys.

　　　　　Seasonal Activities • EMC 2003 • © Evan-Moor Corp.

# Planting Corn

Plant a fish with the corn seeds.

Cut out the pictures. Glue them in order.

| **1** | **2** | **3** |
|---|---|---|
| glue | glue | glue |

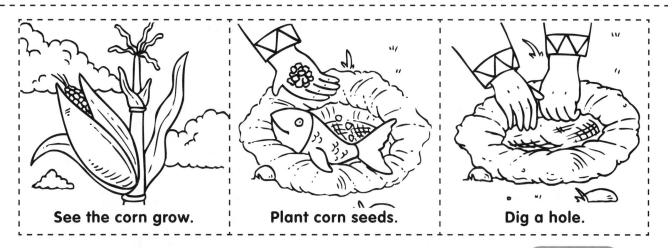

**See the corn grow.**     **Plant corn seeds.**     **Dig a hole.**

# Pilgrim Children

Color the picture. Make a red X in front of what a Pilgrim child would do.
Draw a blue line under what a child today would do.

_____ go to school

_____ watch TV

_____ play with friends

_____ help mother do housework

_____ help father hunt

_____ go to church on Sunday

_____ eat pizza

_____ ride a bus to school

_____ dress like their parents

_____ shop at the mall

Seasonal Activities • EMC 2003 • © Evan-Moor Corp.

Name _____

# New Foods in America

The Pilgrims learned many things in America.
They learned how to hunt animals for food.
They learned how to plant new kinds of food.

Circle the foods the Pilgrims found in America.

```
c  p  e  a  n  u  t  s  d  s
o  t  o  m  a  t  o  r  e  q
r  p  u  m  p  k  i  n  e  u
n  p  o  p  c  o  r  n  r  a
p  o  t  a  t  o  x  z  w  s
l  i  m  a  b  e  a  n  s  h
```

**— Word Box —**

____ corn          ____ peanuts     ____ potato      ____ squash
____ lima beans    ____ popcorn     ____ pumpkin     ____ tomato

Which of these foods have you eaten?

_____

_____

_____

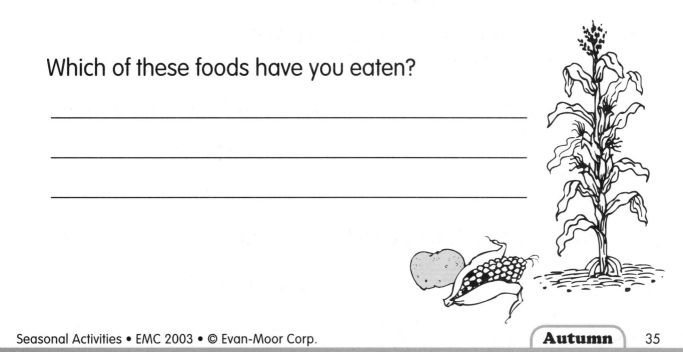

Name _____

# Wild Turkey

Draw the other side. Color the picture.

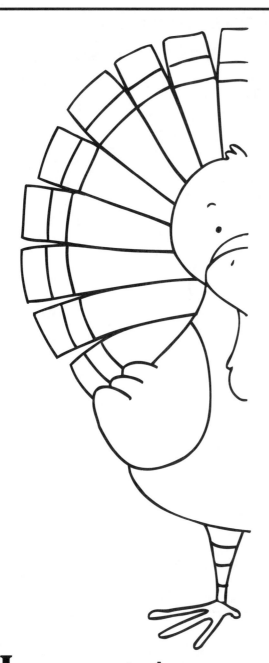

**L**ong ago, turkeys were found only in America.
Early settlers hunted them for food.
Now turkeys are grown on farms.
We buy our turkey at the market.

Seasonal Activities • EMC 2003 • © Evan-Moor Corp.

Name _____

# I Am Thankful

For sunshine and shade.
For games I have played.
For blankets at night.
And bearhugs tight.

Jill Norris

Draw something you are thankful for.

```
┌─────────────────────────────────────┐
│                                     │
│                                     │
│                                     │
│                                     │
│                                     │
│                                     │
│                                     │
│                                     │
│                                     │
└─────────────────────────────────────┘
```

I am thankful for _____

_____

_____

_____ .

Name _____

# Thanksgiving Dinner
# at My House

Draw what you eat for Thanksgiving dinner.

My favorite part of Thanksgiving dinner is _____

_____

_____

_____ .

Seasonal Activities • EMC 2003 • © Evan-Moor Corp.

## Calendars

## Winter Weather

## Winter Holidays

Name _____

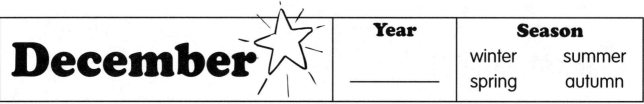

| December | Year | Season |
|----------|------|--------|
| | _____ | winter    summer<br>spring    autumn |

Parents, please post this calendar. Help your children with the items below.

| Sunday | Monday | Tuesday | Wednesday | Thursday | Friday | Saturday |
|--------|--------|---------|-----------|----------|--------|----------|
| | | | | | | |
| | | | | | | |
| | | | | | | |
| | | | | | | |
| | | | | | | |

1. Write the number for each day in December.

2. There are always _____ days in December.

3. Draw a snowman on the first day of winter.

4. Draw a green wreath around Christmas Day.

5. Color each day of winter vacation.

6. Record class birthdays on your calendar.

Seasonal Activities • EMC 2003 • © Evan-Moor Corp.

Name _____

| January  | Year<br>_____ | Season<br>winter    summer<br>spring    autumn |
|---|---|---|

Parents, please post this calendar. Help your children with the items below.

| Sunday | Monday | Tuesday | Wednesday | Thursday | Friday | Saturday |
|---|---|---|---|---|---|---|
|  |  |  |  |  |  |  |
|  |  |  |  |  |  |  |
|  |  |  |  |  |  |  |
|  |  |  |  |  |  |  |
|  |  |  |  |  |  |  |

1. Write the number for each day in January.

2. There are always _____ days in January.

3. Make a big star on New Year's Day.

4. Outline Martin Luther King, Jr.'s birthday.

5. What day of the week is January 16? _____

6. Record class birthdays on your calendar.

Name _____

| February | Year _____ | Season |
|----------|-------------|--------|
|          |             | winter    summer |
|          |             | spring    autumn |

Parents, please post this calendar. Help your children with the items below.

| Sunday | Monday | Tuesday | Wednesday | Thursday | Friday | Saturday |
|--------|--------|---------|-----------|----------|--------|----------|
|        |        |         |           |          |        |          |
|        |        |         |           |          |        |          |
|        |        |         |           |          |        |          |
|        |        |         |           |          |        |          |
|        |        |         |           |          |        |          |

1. Write the number for each day in February.

2. There are usually _____ days in February.

   In leap years there are _____ days.

3. Color Groundhog Day black like a shadow.

4. Draw a red heart on Valentine's Day.

5. Circle the birthdays of George Washington and Abraham Lincoln.

6. Record class birthdays on your calendar.

Name _____

# Winter

Color the picture.

Fill in the blanks.

_____ is the first day of winter.

date

The weather is _____ .

Name —————————————————

# Snowflakes

Draw lines to match the snowflakes that are alike.

Does it snow where you live?    yes        no

Seasonal Activities • EMC 2003 • © Evan-Moor Corp.

Name ————————————

# Snowy Day

Color the picture. Answer the question.

**I**t's snowing! It's snowing!
Let's go out to play.
Put on mittens.
Grab your scarf.
We'll have fun today!

What would you do on a snowy day?

————————————————————————

————————————————————————

————————————————————————

Name _____

# Snowy Word Search

Find the words. Circle them.

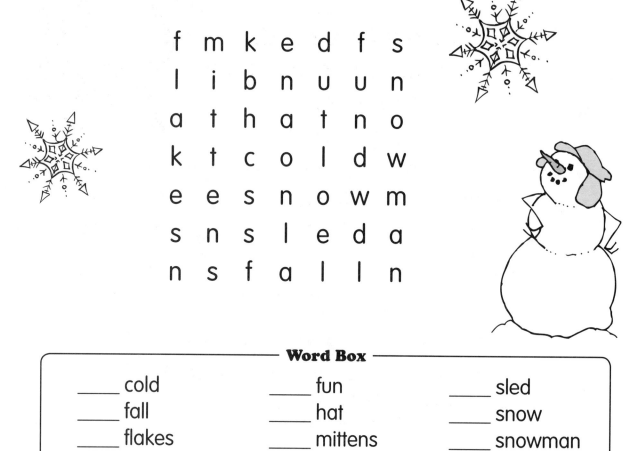

```
f  m  k  e  d  f  s
l  i  b  n  u  u  n
a  t  h  a  t  n  o
k  t  c  o  l  d  w
e  e  s  n  o  w  m
s  n  s  l  e  d  a
n  s  f  a  l  l  n
```

## Word Box

_____ cold        _____ fun        _____ sled
_____ fall        _____ hat        _____ snow
_____ flakes      _____ mittens    _____ snowman

Fill in the missing words.

1. I put on my _____ and _____ to
   play in the snow.

2. I rode my _____ down the hill.

3. Snow_____ fell from the sky.

4. I made a big _____ in the backyard.

Seasonal Activities • EMC 2003 • © Evan-Moor Corp.

Name _____

# A Riddle

Use the code to answer the riddle.

We fall from the sky.
We are white and fluffy.
What are we?

| 1 = a | 4 = k | 7 = o |
|-------|-------|-------|
| 2 = e | 5 = l | 8 = s |
| 3 = f | 6 = n | 9 = w |

| 4<br>+4<br>---<br>8<br>s | 3<br>+3<br>--- | 5<br>+2<br>--- | 6<br>+3<br>--- |
|-----|-----|-----|-----|
|  |  |  |  |

| 2<br>+1<br>--- | 3<br>+2<br>--- | 1<br>+0<br>--- | 2<br>+2<br>--- | 1<br>+1<br>--- | 5<br>+3<br>--- |
|-----|-----|-----|-----|-----|-----|
|  |  |  |  |  |  |

Name _____

# Winter Words

Write the name of each picture.

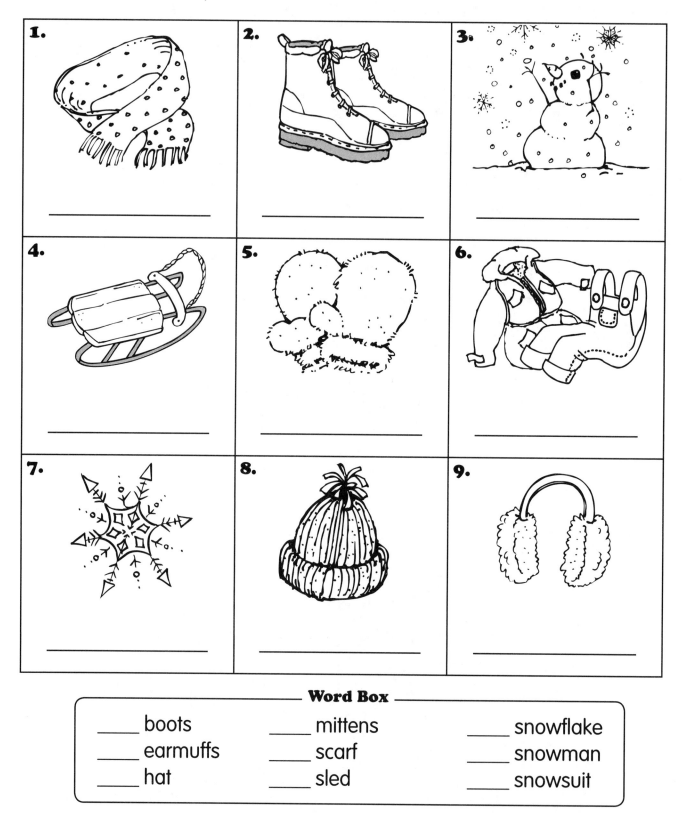

1.

2.

3.

4.

5.

6.

7.

8.

9.

**Word Box**

| ____ boots | ____ mittens | ____ snowflake |
| ____ earmuffs | ____ scarf | ____ snowman |
| ____ hat | ____ sled | ____ snowsuit |

Seasonal Activities • EMC 2003 • © Evan-Moor Corp.

Name _____

# My Snowman

Draw the other side of the snowman. Color the picture.

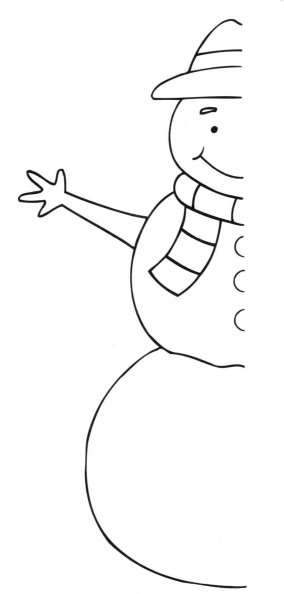

Unscramble the words to make a sentence. Draw what it says about the snowman.

| nose. | My | has | carrot | snowman | a | chubby |
|-------|-----|-----|--------|---------|---|--------|

_____

_____ .

Name _____

# Snow Words

Write the missing part of the word to name the picture.

snow_____     snow_____     snow_____

snow_____     snow_____     snow_____

**Word Box**

____ ball          ____ man           ____ shoe
____ flake         ____ mobile        ____ suit

Fill in the missing word in the sentence.

1. I rode a _____ with my dad.

2. Did the _____ have a carrot nose?

3. Can you hit the pole with a _____?

**Note:** Reproduce pages 51 and 52 for this little book.

# Winter Holidays

Cut on the lines.
Put the pages in order.
Staple the pages together.

staple

# Winter Holidays

by Jill Norris

1

## *Celebrating Christmas*

The candles are lit.
The cooking is done.
Carolers are singing.
Let's all have some fun.

2

### Celebrating Kwanzaa

Remember the past and
live responsibly today.
The candles on the kinara
tell us the way.

3

### Celebrating La Posada

Candles twinkle
along the way
As we look for
a place to stay.

INN

4

### Celebrating Hanukkah

Add one candle
every night.
The menorah spreads
a special light.

5

Name _____

# The Christmas Story

Color the picture.

**M**ary had a baby. His name was Jesus.
Three wise men brought gifts for baby Jesus.

Draw a line to make a match.

Jesus was                    baby Jesus's mother.

Mary was                     a baby.

There were                   brought gifts.

The wise men                 three wise men.

# A Family Celebration

Color the pictures. Answer the question.

On Christmas morning, we go to church.

After church, my family unwraps our presents.

Does your family have a Christmas celebration?     yes     no

Seasonal Activities • EMC 2003 • © Evan-Moor Corp.

# Three Wise Men

The Three Wise Men are looking for baby Jesus.
Draw a line to help them find their way.

Name _____

# Christmas Surprise

Fill in the words to find the Christmas surprise.
Draw the surprise on the back of this paper.

**Word Box**

____ card
____ December
____ elf
____ gift
____ holly
____ reindeer
____ Santa Claus
____ sleigh
____ snow
____ wreath

Seasonal Activities • EMC 2003 • © Evan-Moor Corp.

# Santa's Reindeer

Look who is ready to pull Santa's sleigh.
Follow the steps to draw one of Santa's reindeer. Color the picture.

What is the reindeer's name? _____

Name _____

# More Than One

Write the word that names
more than one of each thing.

Word Box

____ boxes
____ children
____ deer
____ feet
____ geese
____ gifts
____ men
____ mice
____ sleighs
____ teeth

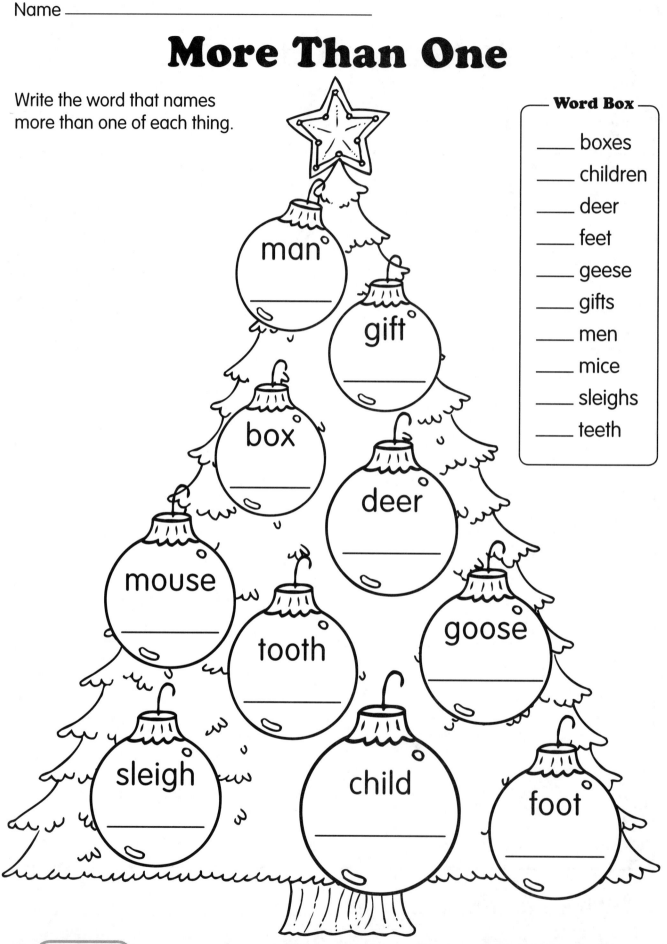

man° _____

gift° _____

box° _____

deer _____

mouse _____

tooth _____

goose _____

sleigh _____

child _____

foot _____

Seasonal Activities • EMC 2003 • © Evan-Moor Corp.

Name _____

# Reindeer and Elves

Use the reindeer and elf to help
you find the answers.
Draw the answer to each question.
Then count and write the answer.

1. How many legs do
   two reindeer and
   one elf have in all?

   [ ] legs

2. How many tails do
   three reindeer and
   two elves have in all?

   [ ] tails

3. How many ears do
   three elves and two
   reindeer have in all?

   [ ] ears

Name _____

# What Is It?

Start at **1**. Connect the dots.
Color the picture.

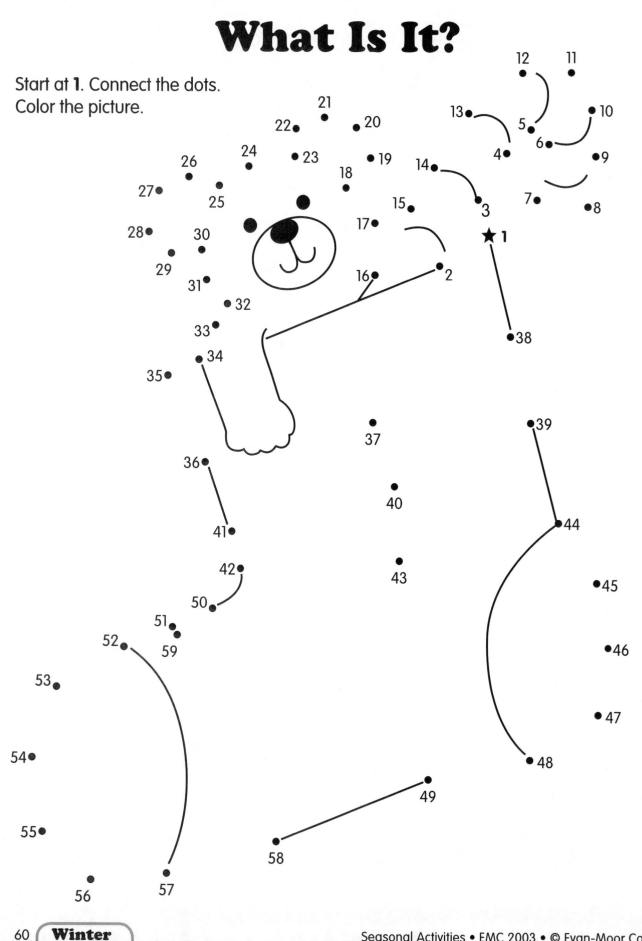

Seasonal Activities • EMC 2003 • © Evan-Moor Corp.

Name _____

# Riddle Time

Use the code to answer the riddles.

Why does Rudolph need
an umbrella?

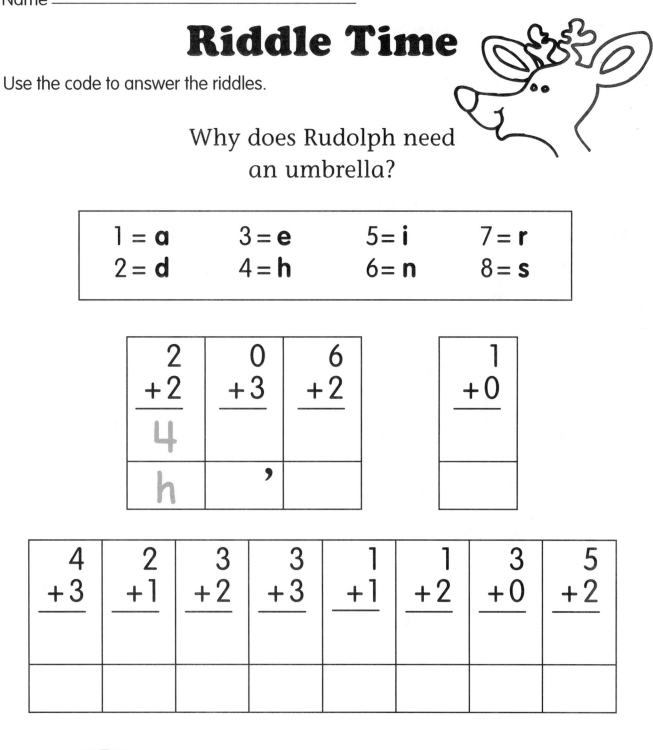

| 1 = **a** | 3 = **e** | 5 = **i** | 7 = **r** |
| 2 = **d** | 4 = **h** | 6 = **n** | 8 = **s** |

$$\begin{array}{c} 2 \\ +2 \\ \hline 4 \\ h \end{array} \quad \begin{array}{c} 0 \\ +3 \\ \hline , \end{array} \quad \begin{array}{c} 6 \\ +2 \\ \hline \end{array} \qquad \begin{array}{c} 1 \\ +0 \\ \hline \end{array}$$

$$\begin{array}{c} 4 \\ +3 \\ \hline \end{array} \quad \begin{array}{c} 2 \\ +1 \\ \hline \end{array} \quad \begin{array}{c} 3 \\ +2 \\ \hline \end{array} \quad \begin{array}{c} 3 \\ +3 \\ \hline \end{array} \quad \begin{array}{c} 1 \\ +1 \\ \hline \end{array} \quad \begin{array}{c} 1 \\ +2 \\ \hline \end{array} \quad \begin{array}{c} 3 \\ +0 \\ \hline \end{array} \quad \begin{array}{c} 5 \\ +2 \\ \hline \end{array}$$

When do you need an umbrella?

_____

_____

_____

# Hanukkah

Read the story. Color the picture.

**J**ewish families get together each night of Hanukkah. They light the menorah. It holds the candles they light each night. Two candles are lit the first night. One more candle is lit each night. On the eighth night, all of the candles are lit.

Make a match.

| | |
|---|---|
| The menorah has | a Jewish holiday. |
| On the first night, | nine candles. |
| Hanukkah is | two candles are lit. |

Name _____

# A Family Celebration

Color the picture. Answer the questions.

**M**y family has a special feast for Hanukkah.
We play games and sing. We eat special foods. Children
receive money and play with tops called dreidels.

Does your family celebrate Hanukkah?          yes          no

Have you ever played with a dreidel?          yes          no

# Spin, Dreidel, Spin

Connect the dots. Start at **0** and count by **10s**. Color the picture.

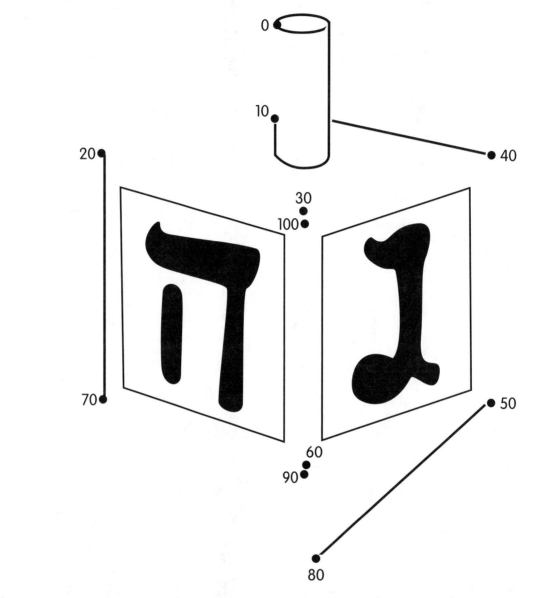

The four sides of a dreidel:

| Shin | Heh | Gimmel | Nun |
|------|-----|--------|-----|
| Put one token in the pot. | Take half of the tokens in the pot. | Take the whole pot. | Miss the turn. |

Seasonal Activities • EMC 2003 • © Evan-Moor Corp.

# Kwanzaa

Read the story. Color the candles **r**ed, **b**lack, and **g**reen.

**K**wanzaa is an African-American holiday. Kwanzaa celebrates family history. It lasts for seven days. Each day has a special meaning to think about. A candle is lit on a kinara every day.

Make a match.

Kwanzaa lasts                  their history.

A kinara has                   a special meaning to think about.

Families celebrate             seven candles.

Each day has                   seven days.

Name _____

# A Family Celebration

Color the picture. Answer the question.

**M**y family celebrates Kwanzaa for seven days. We share stories about our family history. We eat, sing, and play music. Children get African or homemade gifts.

Does your family celebrate Kwanzaa?          yes          no

Name _____

# A New Year

There are twelve months in a year.

Start at **January**. Connect the dots.

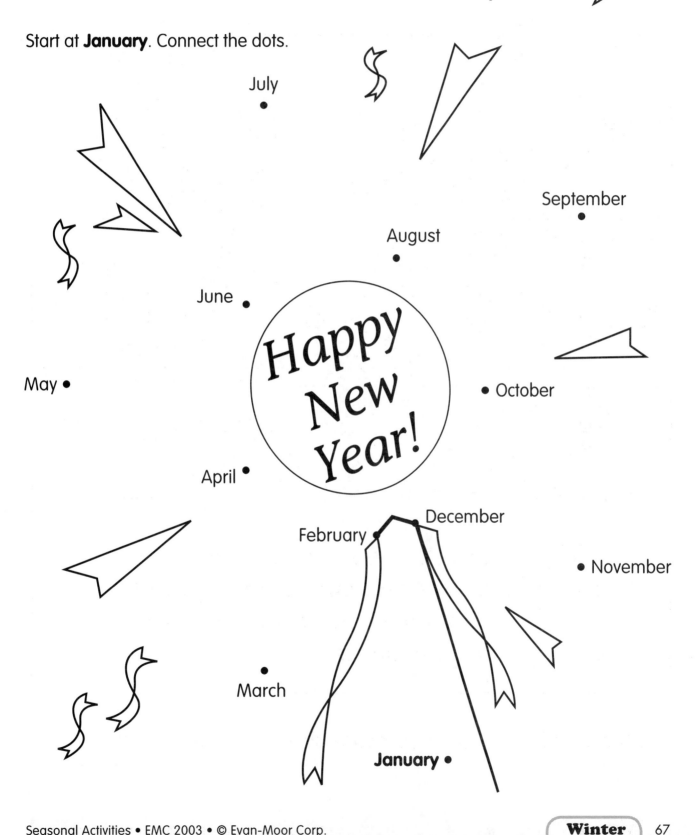

July

September

August

June

May

Happy New Year!

October

April

December

February

November

March

January

Name _____

# The Months of the Year

Write the name of each month in the correct order.

| J | a | n | u | a | r | y | has _____ days.

[ ][ ][ ][ ][ ][ ][ ][ ] has _____ days.

[ ][ ][ ][ ][ ][ ] has _____ days.

[ ][ ][ ][ ][ ][ ] has _____ days.

[ ][ ][ ] has _____ days.

[ ][ ][ ][ ] has _____ days.

[ ][ ][ ][ ] has _____ days.

[ ][ ][ ][ ][ ][ ] has _____ days.

[ ][ ][ ][ ][ ][ ][ ][ ][ ] has _____ days.

[ ][ ][ ][ ][ ][ ][ ] has _____ days.

[ ][ ][ ][ ][ ][ ][ ][ ] has _____ days.

[ ][ ][ ][ ][ ][ ][ ][ ] has _____ days.

**Word Box**

____ April
____ August
____ December
____ February
____ January
____ July
____ June
____ March
____ May
____ November
____ October
____ September

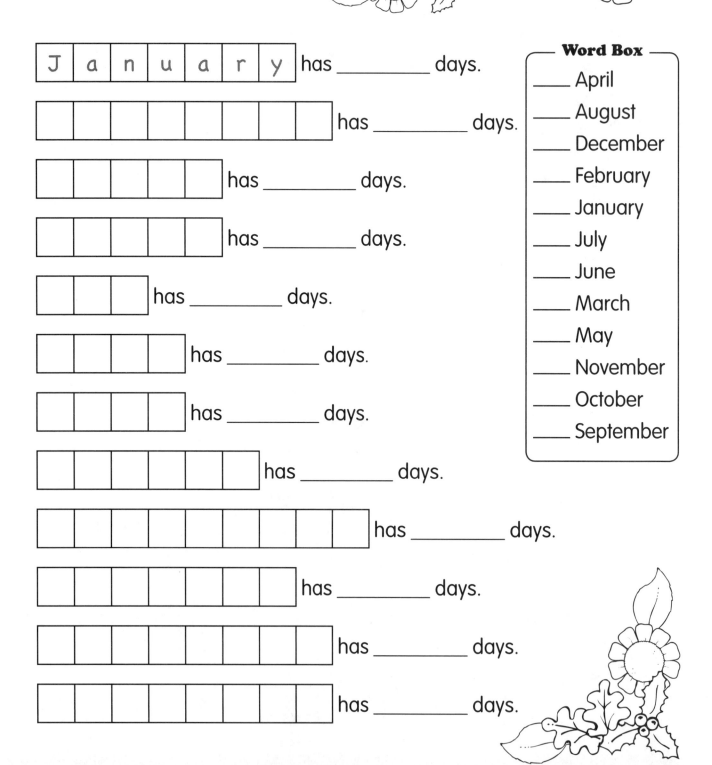

Seasonal Activities • EMC 2003 • © Evan-Moor Corp.

Name _____

# Martin Luther King, Jr., Day

Cut out the pieces. Glue them to finish the picture.

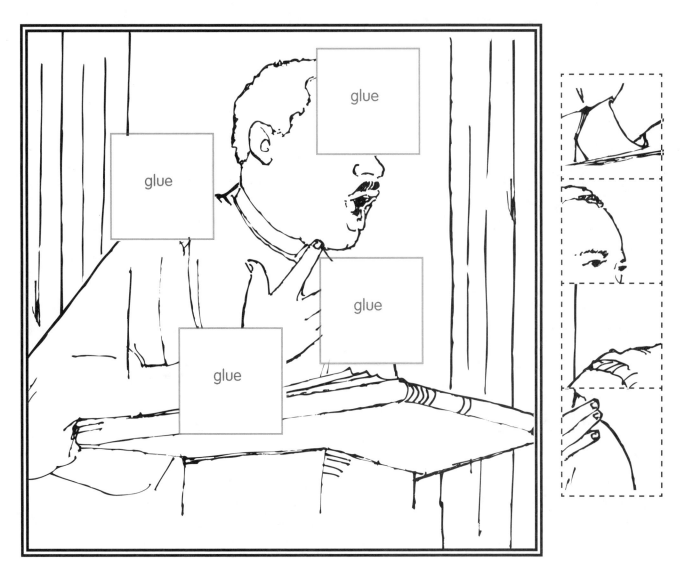

**T**his is a day to celebrate a hero. Martin Luther King, Jr., wanted everyone to be treated fairly.

- He led marches.
- He gave speeches.
- He worked to change laws.

He helped to make the world a better place.

# Martin Luther King, Jr.

Name _____

Color the picture.

He had a special dream.
He worked to make it true.
He did it for all people
Including me and you.

Jill Norris

Seasonal Activities • EMC 2003 • © Evan-Moor Corp.

# Groundhog Day

Read the story. Answer the questions.

**D**o you think a groundhog can tell what the weather will be? An old story says that this can happen. If the groundhog sees his shadow when he comes out of his winter den, there will be six more weeks of winter. If he doesn't see his shadow, spring will be early.

**Will spring be early?**

yes        no

**Will spring be early?**

yes        no

Name _____

# Groundhog's Shadow

Draw a line to match each groundhog to its shadow.

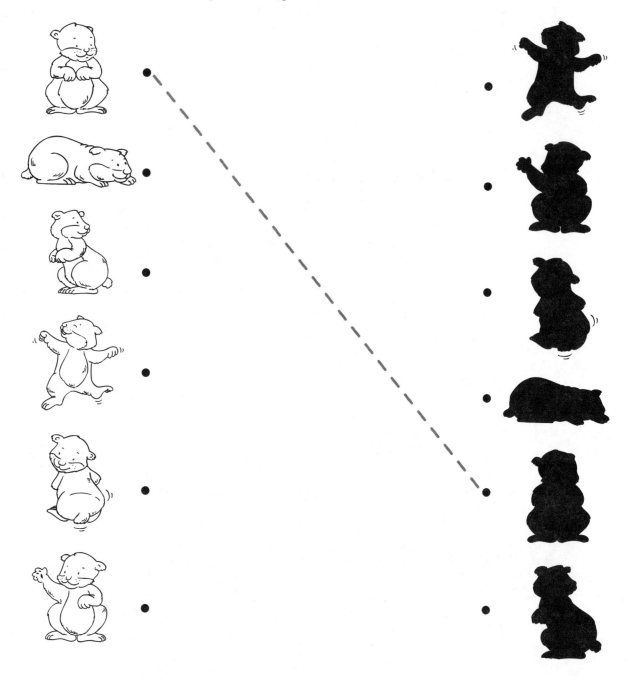

When Groundhog sees his shadow _____

_____

_____.

Name _____

# Chinese New Year

Color the dragon.

**A** big parade is held for Chinese New Year. A fierce dragon dances along the parade. The dragon chases away bad luck. Noisy firecrackers are set off, too.

# Presidents' Day

Cut on the lines. Put the pages in order. Staple them together.

staple

Presidents' Day

George Washington was our first president.

1

Abraham Lincoln was our 16th president.

2

They helped to make our country the place we know today.

3

In February, we celebrate their birthdays on Presidents' Day.

4

Seasonal Activities • EMC 2003 • © Evan-Moor Corp.

Name _____

# George Washington

**G**eorge Washington was born on February 22 in Virginia. He became the first president of the United States of America.

Draw the other side. Color the picture.

Why do you think he is called the "Father of Our Country"?

_____

_____

# Abraham Lincoln

**A**braham Lincoln was born on February 12 in Kentucky. He was the 16th president of the United States of America.

Circle the numbers 1 through 16 with a red crayon.

Why do you think he was called "Honest Abe"?

_____

_____

Seasonal Activities • EMC 2003 • © Evan-Moor Corp.

Name _____

# Valentine's Day

Draw a line to match the two sides of each valentine.

**V**alentine's Day is a time for friends.
It is a time to share cards and candy.

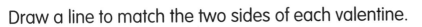 Draw a valentine for a friend on the back of this paper.

# Where Are the Hearts?

Find the hidden hearts. Color them.

How many hearts did you find? ☐

Seasonal Activities • EMC 2003 • © Evan-Moor Corp.

# Contractions

Read the contractions. Write the words.

it's     <u>it is</u>

won't     _____

I'm     _____

isn't     _____

didn't     _____

they're     _____

he'll     _____

I've     _____

can't     _____

she's     _____

## Word Box

| ___ can not | ___ did not | ___ he will | ___ I am | ___ I have |
|---|---|---|---|---|
| ✔ it is | ___ they are | ___ will not | ___ is not | ___ she is |

Name

# Delivering Valentines

Help deliver the valentines.

Unscramble the message.
Then write it below.

| valentine? | be | you | my | Will |

_____

Seasonal Activities • EMC 2003 • © Evan-Moor Corp.

**Spring**

### Calendars

### Spring Weather

### Spring Holidays

### Easter

### May Holidays

### Mother's Day

Name _____

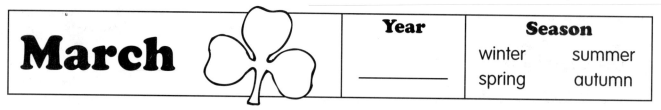

# March

| | Year | Season |
|---|---|---|
| | _____ | winter     summer<br>spring     autumn |

Parents, please post this calendar. Help your children with the items below.

| Sunday | Monday | Tuesday | Wednesday | Thursday | Friday | Saturday |
|---|---|---|---|---|---|---|
| | | | | | | |
| | | | | | | |
| | | | | | | |
| | | | | | | |
| | | | | | | |

1. Write the number for each day in March.

2. There are always _____ days in March.

3. Draw a flower on the first day of spring.

4. Circle each Friday in March.

5. Draw a shamrock on Saint Patrick's Day.

6. Record class birthdays on your calendar.

Name _____

| April 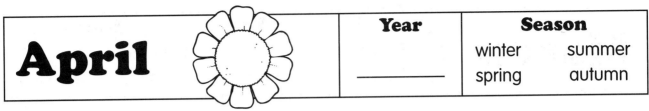 | Year _____ | Season |
|---|---|---|
| | | winter     summer |
| | | spring     autumn |

Parents, please post this calendar. Help your children with the items below.

| Sunday | Monday | Tuesday | Wednesday | Thursday | Friday | Saturday |
|---|---|---|---|---|---|---|
| | | | | | | |
| | | | | | | |
| | | | | | | |
| | | | | | | |
| | | | | | | |

1. Write the number for each day in April.

2. There are always _____ days in April.

3. Which day of the week is April 1? _____

4. Is Easter in April this year?  yes  no

5. How many Wednesdays are in April? _____

6. Record class birthdays on your calendar.

Name _____

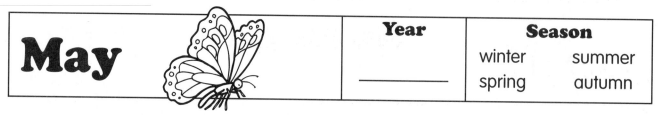

| **May** | **Year** | **Season** |
|---|---|---|
| | _____ | winter summer<br>spring autumn |

Parents, please post this calendar. Help your children with the items below.

| **Sunday** | **Monday** | **Tuesday** | **Wednesday** | **Thursday** | **Friday** | **Saturday** |
|---|---|---|---|---|---|---|
| | | | | | | |
| | | | | | | |
| | | | | | | |
| | | | | | | |
| | | | | | | |

1. Write the number for each day in May.

2. There are always _____ days in May.

3. Outline Mother's Day with your favorite color.

4. Draw a basket of spring flowers on May Day.

5. How many Sundays are there in May? _____

6. Record class birthdays on your calendar.

Seasonal Activities • EMC 2003 • © Evan-Moor Corp.

Name _____

# Spring

Color the picture.

Fill in the blanks.

_____ is the first day of spring.
date

The weather is _____ .

Name _____

# It Rhymes with "Spring"

Add **ing** to each word. Read the words. Draw a line to the correct picture.

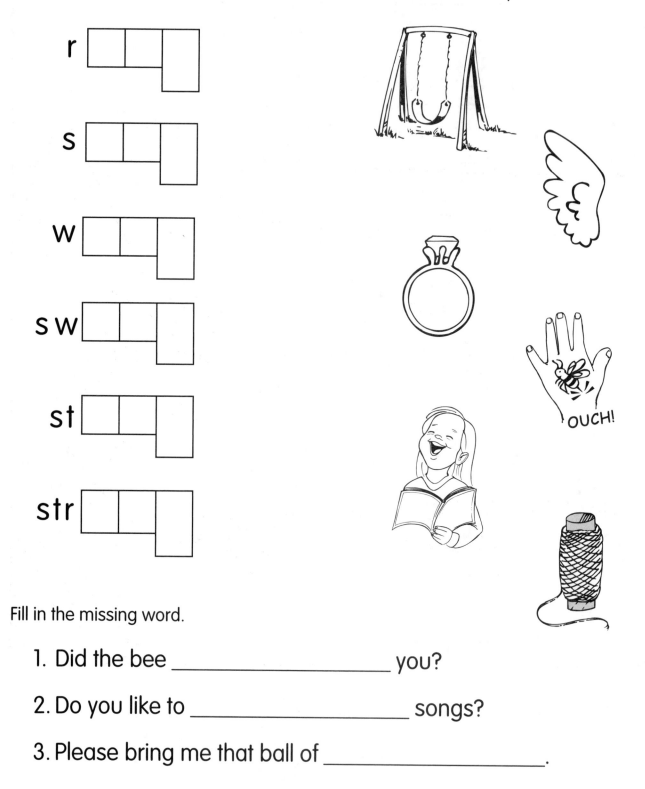

r ☐☐☐

s ☐☐☐

w ☐☐☐

s w ☐☐☐

s t ☐☐☐

s t r ☐☐☐

Fill in the missing word.

1. Did the bee _____ you?

2. Do you like to _____ songs?

3. Please bring me that ball of _____.

Seasonal Activities • EMC 2003 • © Evan-Moor Corp.

Name _____

# A Windy Day

Color the picture. Answer the question.

Wind's blowing! Wind's blowing!
    Let's go out to play.
    Put on a sweater.
    Grab your kite.
We'll have fun today.

What would you do on a windy day? _____

_____

_____

Name _____

# April Showers

Draw the other side. Add raindrops falling from the clouds. Color the picture.

Rain is water that falls from the clouds.
A cloud is made of millions of little drops of water.
When a cloud gets full of water, raindrops begin to fall.

Seasonal Activities • EMC 2003 • © Evan-Moor Corp.

Name _____

# It's Raining!

Find the rainy day words in the word search.
Circle the words you find.

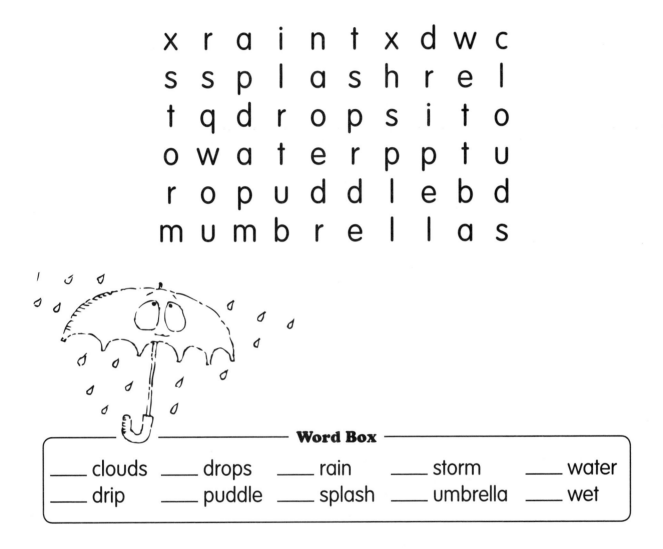

x r a i n t x d w c
s s p l a s h r e l
t q d r o p s i t o
o w a t e r p p t u
r o p u d d l e b d
m u m b r e l l a s

**Word Box**

| | | | | |
|---|---|---|---|---|
| ___ clouds | ___ drops | ___ rain | ___ storm | ___ water |
| ___ drip | ___ puddle | ___ splash | ___ umbrella | ___ wet |

Fill in the missing words.

1. The _____ were dark.

2. It started to _____.

3. The _____ of _____ fell

   on my _____.

# Rainbow

Draw a rainbow and color it.
What colors will you use?

When rain falls down
And the sun shines behind,
You can see a rainbow,
It's easy to find!

I see red, orange, yellow,
green, blue, and purple
in the rainbow.

Name _____

# Dress for a Rainy Day

Connect the dots, counting by **5s**. Color the picture.

Name _____

# Rainy Day Words

Write the words on the lines.

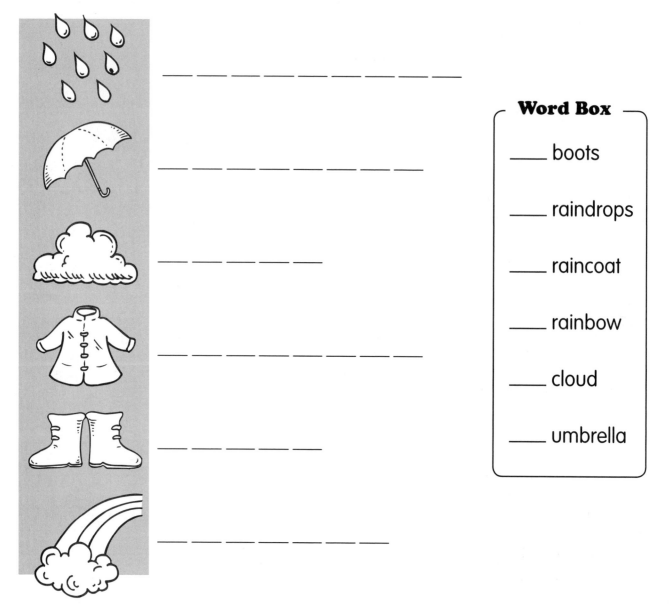

— — — — — — — — — — — —

— — — — — — — — — —

— — — — — — — —

— — — — — — — — — — —

— — — — — — —

— — — — — — — —

Now use the words above to fill in the blanks.

1. I have _____ on my feet.

2. The _____ are falling from the sky.

3. My _____ will keep the rain off my head.

4. A colorful _____ lit up the sky.

Name _____

# Spring Flowers

**F**lowers make the seeds that grow into new plants.

Unscramble the letters to name the flowers.
Draw a line to make a match. Color the flowers.

f o d a f d i l _____

e s o r _____

a i s d y _____

l u t i p _____

a n p s y _____

f l o w s u n e r _____

**Word Box**

____ rose     ____ daffodil     ____ pansy
____ daisy     ____ tulip     ____ sunflower

What would you grow in your flower garden?

_____

Name _____

# A Pea Plant Grows

Cut and glue the pictures in order.

| 1 | 2 | 3 |
|---|---|---|
| glue | glue | glue |

| 4 | 5 | 6 |
|---|---|---|
| glue | glue | glue |

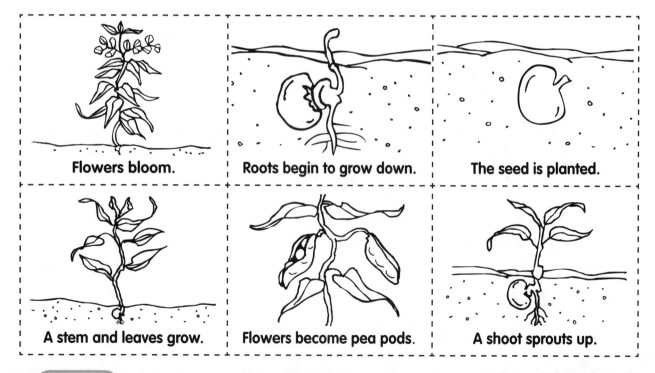

Flowers bloom.

Roots begin to grow down.

The seed is planted.

A stem and leaves grow.

Flowers become pea pods.

A shoot sprouts up.

Seasonal Activities • EMC 2003 • © Evan-Moor Corp.

Name _____

# In the Garden

Start at **A**.
Connect the dots.
Color the picture.

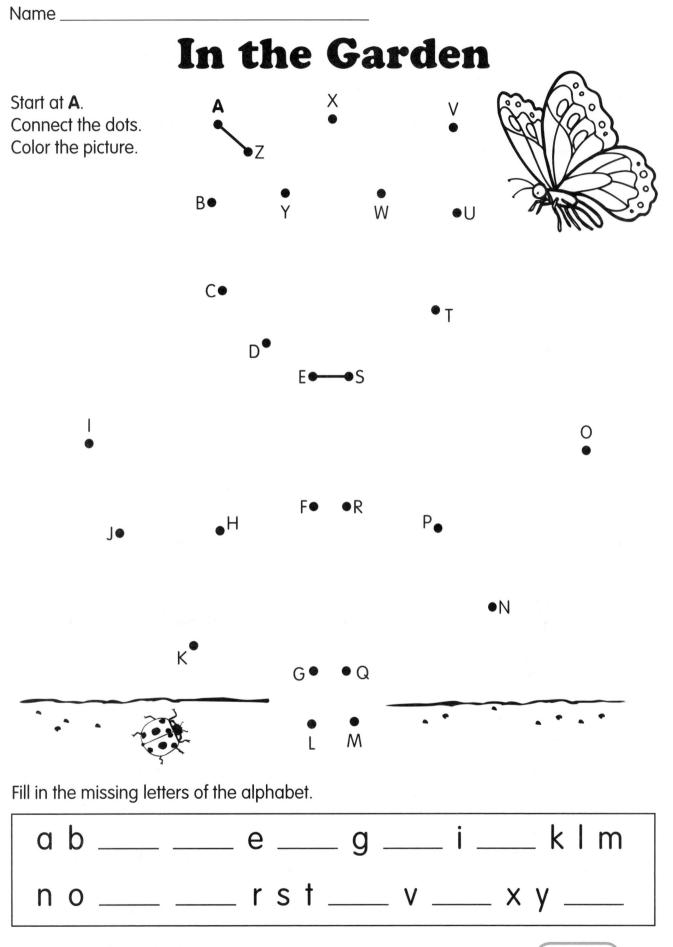

Fill in the missing letters of the alphabet.

a b ___ ___ e ___ g ___ i ___ k l m

n o ___ ___ r s t ___ v ___ x y ___

Name _____

Note: Reproduce the pictures on page 97 to use with this activity.

# A Butterfly Grows

Cut out the pictures on page 97. Glue them in order on the chart below.

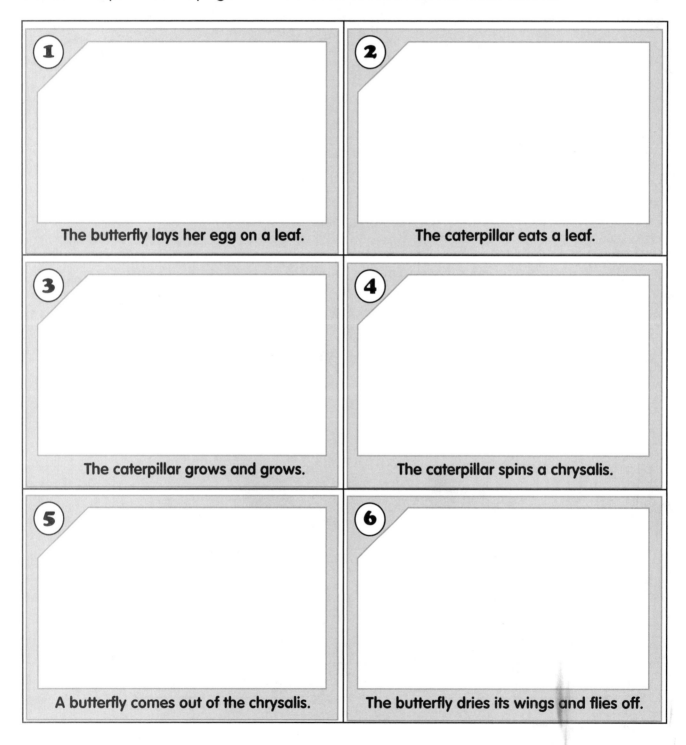

| | |
|---|---|
| **1** | **2** |
| The butterfly lays her egg on a leaf. | The caterpillar eats a leaf. |
| **3** | **4** |
| The caterpillar grows and grows. | The caterpillar spins a chrysalis. |
| **5** | **6** |
| A butterfly comes out of the chrysalis. | The butterfly dries its wings and flies off. |

**Note:** Reproduce these pictures to sequence on page 96.

Color and then cut out these pictures. Glue them in order on page 96.

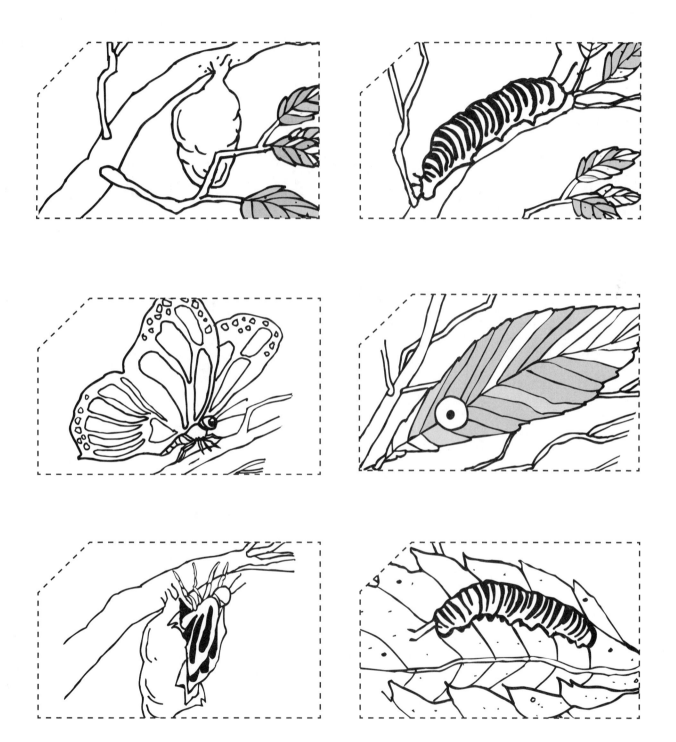

Name _____

# May Flowers

Find the word that is the opposite.
Write it on the correct flower.

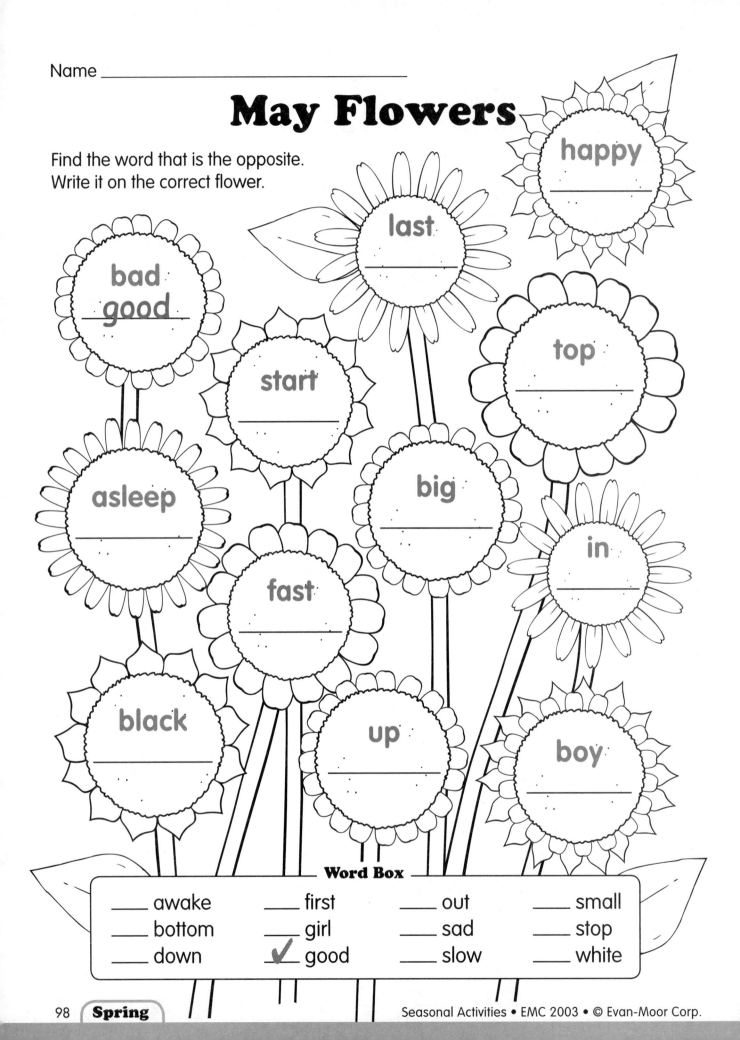

happy
_____

last
_____

bad
good
_____

top
_____

start
_____

asleep
_____

big
_____

in
_____

fast
_____

black
_____

up
_____

boy
_____

**Word Box**

| | | | |
|---|---|---|---|
| ___ awake | ___ first | ___ out | ___ small |
| ___ bottom | ___ girl | ___ sad | ___ stop |
| ___ down | ✔ good | ___ slow | ___ white |

Seasonal Activities • EMC 2003 • © Evan-Moor Corp.

Name _____

# Earth Day

Connect the dots. Start at **5** and count by **5s**. Color the land green. Color the water blue.

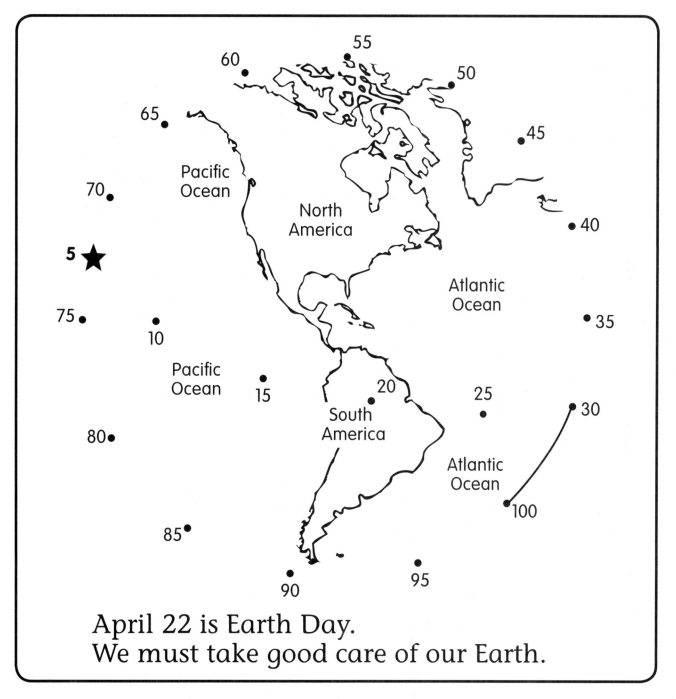

What can you do to take care of the Earth?

_____

_____

Name _____

# Clean Up the Earth

Color the picture.

Don't be a litterbug.
Pick up litter to keep the Earth clean.
Put the litter in the garbage can.

How many words can you make out of the letters in **trash**?

_____ _____ _____ _____

          Seasonal Activities • EMC 2003 • © Evan-Moor Corp.

# Johnny Appleseed

Color, then cut on the lines. Put the pages in order. Staple them together.

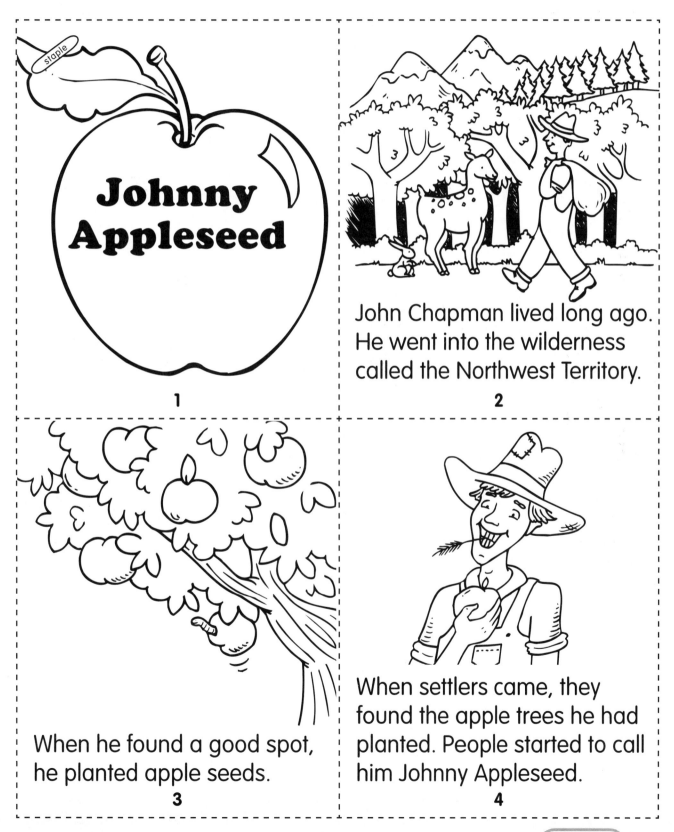

staple

**Johnny Appleseed**

1

John Chapman lived long ago. He went into the wilderness called the Northwest Territory.

2

When he found a good spot, he planted apple seeds.

3

When settlers came, they found the apple trees he had planted. People started to call him Johnny Appleseed.

4

Name _____

# Picking Apples

How many apples did Johnny Appleseed pick? Add the apples together to see.

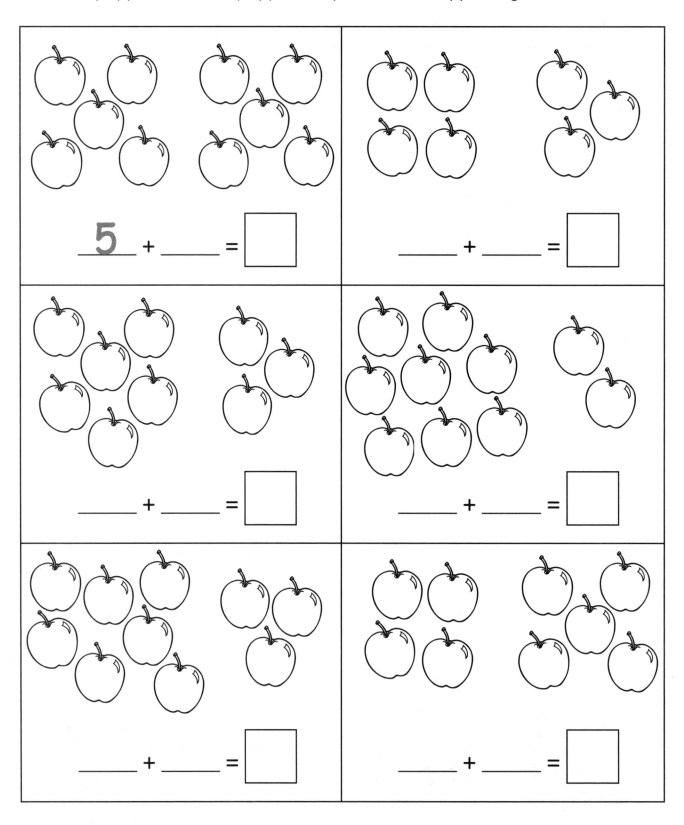

Seasonal Activities • EMC 2003 • © Evan-Moor Corp.

Name _____

# Apple Pie

One way to eat apples is in apple pie.

Cut out the pictures. Glue them in order. Write about each picture.

| | | |
|---|---|---|
| **1** | glue | _____ <br> _____ <br> _____ |
| **2** | glue | _____ <br> _____ <br> _____ |
| **3** | glue | _____ <br> _____ <br> _____ |
| **4** | glue | _____ <br> _____ <br> _____ |

# Saint Patrick's Day

Saint Patrick's Day is an Irish celebration. Saint Patrick lived a long time ago in Ireland. Today, there are parades on Saint Patrick's Day. Many people wear green. They eat Irish foods like corned beef. You don't have to be Irish to have fun on Saint Patrick's Day.

Count by **2s** to find the lucky four-leaf clover.

Seasonal Activities • EMC 2003 • © Evan-Moor Corp.

# Leprechaun

Follow the steps to draw a leprechaun.

**A** leprechaun is a magical little person in Irish stories. Some stories say that if you catch a leprechaun, he has to give you his pot of gold.

Color the leprechaun's suit green.
Make his hair orange. Draw a pot of gold next to the leprechaun.

Name _____

# Easter Sunday

Start at **A**. Connect the dots.

**E**aster Sunday is an important
day to Christians.
They go to church for special
Easter services.

Seasonal Activities • EMC 2003 • © Evan-Moor Corp.

# Mystery Animal

Fill in the boxes with the names of the pictures. Read the words down the middle of the puzzle to find the mystery animal.

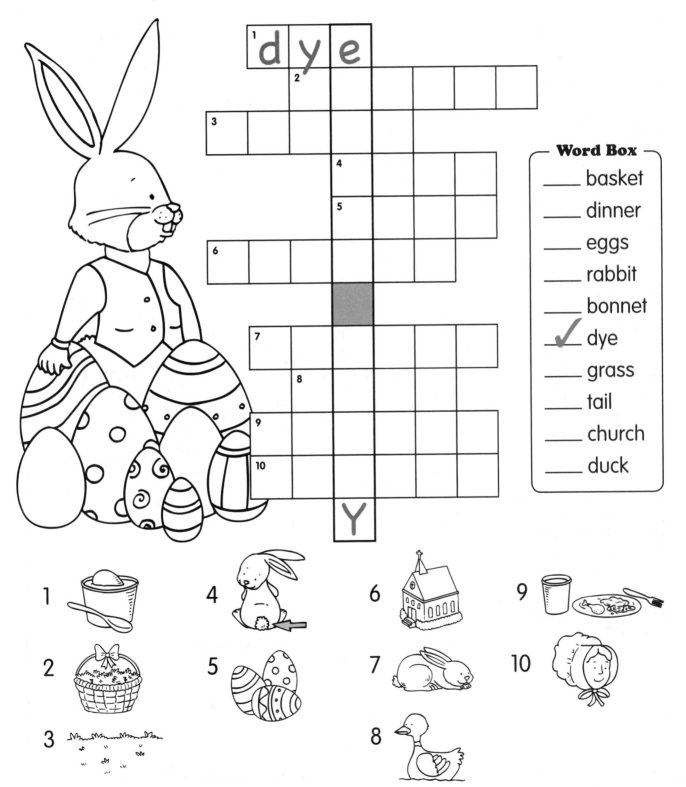

**Word Box**

____ basket

____ dinner

____ eggs

____ rabbit

____ bonnet

✓ dye

____ grass

____ tail

____ church

____ duck

# How to Dye an Easter Egg

Cut out the sentences below. Glue them in order in the numbered boxes.

**1** glue

**2** glue

**3** glue

**4** glue

Put eggs in the cups. Turn the eggs with a spoon.

Get cups and spoons. Set them on the table.

Lift the eggs out and let them dry.

Put dye in each cup. Add water and vinegar. Stir.

# Unscramble the Eggs

Unscramble the color words.
Then color the Easter eggs.

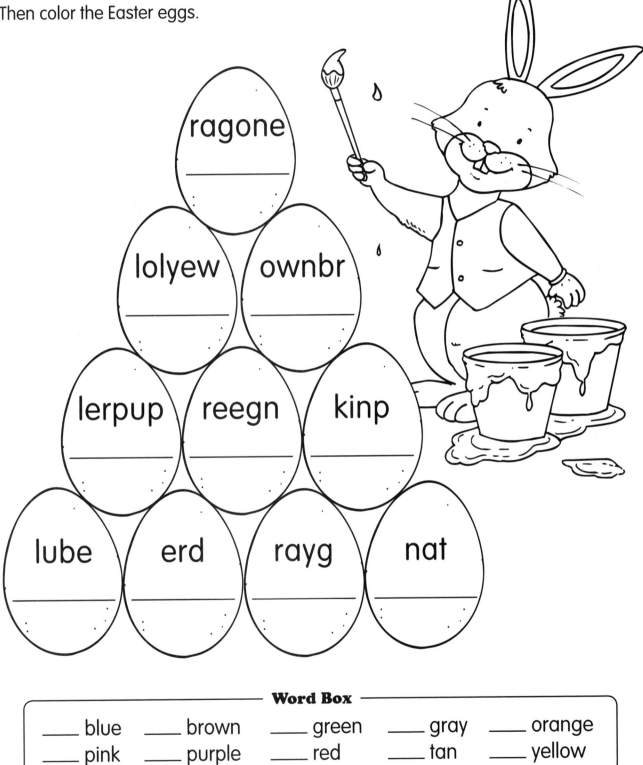

ragone

_____

lolyew

_____

ownbr

_____

lerpup

_____

reegn

_____

kinp

_____

lube

_____

erd

_____

rayg

_____

nat

_____

**Word Box**

| ___ blue | ___ brown | ___ green | ___ gray | ___ orange |
|----------|-----------|-----------|----------|------------|
| ___ pink | ___ purple | ___ red | ___ tan | ___ yellow |

# Cheep! Cheep!

Draw the other side of the chick and egg. Color the picture.

What is happening in the picture?

_____

_____

Name _____

# Here Comes the Easter Bunny

Color the boxes that say **egg** to make a path for the Easter Bunny.

| | | | |
|---|---|---|---|
| egg | egg | bunny | basket |
| basket | egg | egg | egg |
| candy | bunny | flower | egg |
| egg | egg | egg | egg |
| egg | flower | bunny | candy |
| egg | egg | egg | egg |

How many times did you find **egg**? ☐

Name _____

# Fiesta!

Cut out the pieces. Glue them to finish the puzzle.

glue

glue

glue

glue

**P**eople come to the fiesta
to celebrate Cinco de Mayo.

Seasonal Activities • EMC 2003 • © Evan-Moor Corp.

Name _____

# Piñatas

Color the piñatas. Answer the questions.

**P**iñatas first came from Mexico. They were animal or star shapes. The piñatas were filled with tasty treats. A piñata was hung up high. Children tried to hit the piñata with a stick. When the piñata broke, the treats fell to the ground. Children picked up the treats.

Now piñatas are found in many lands. They are made in all kinds of shapes and sizes. Children still try to break the piñata and pick up the tasty treats.

Have you ever played the piñata game?      yes      no

What tasty treats fell out of the piñata? _____

_____

# May Day

Draw flowers in the basket.

Who would you surprise with a basket of flowers? Tell why.

_____

_____

Seasonal Activities • EMC 2003 • © Evan-Moor Corp.

Name _____

# Maypole Dance

Start at **1**. Connect the dots. Color the picture.

Set up the Maypole.
Take a pretty ribbon.
Dance in and out.
Dance all about.
Spring is here!

# May Basket

Color and cut out the basket. Fold it. Glue the sides together. Punch holes.
Add a strip of yarn for a handle. Put the flowers in your basket.

Seasonal Activities • EMC 2003 • © Evan-Moor Corp.

**Note:** Reproduce this page to use with the May basket on page 116.

Color and cut out the pieces. Put the flowers in your basket.

Happy
May Day!

Happy
May Day!

Happy
May Day!

Happy
May Day!

Name _____

# About My Mother

Draw a picture of your mother. Then write about her.

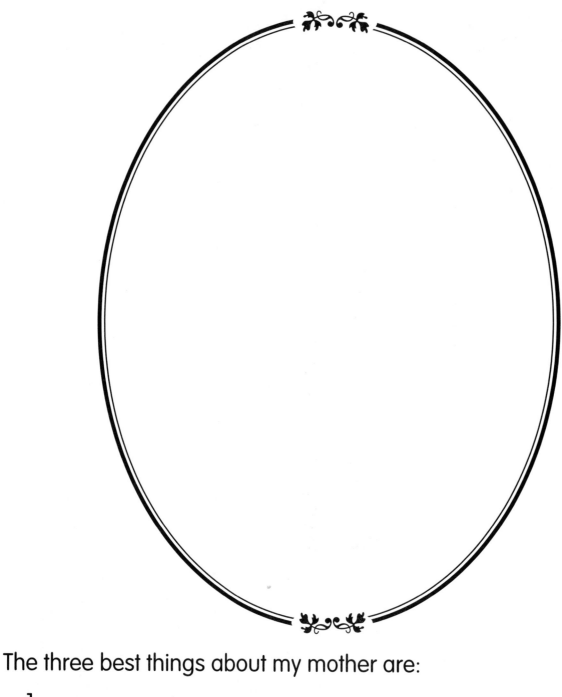

The three best things about my mother are:

1. _____

2. _____

3. _____

Seasonal Activities • EMC 2003 • © Evan-Moor Corp.

# Happy Mother's Day

Color and cut out the card. Fold on the lines. Give it to your mother.

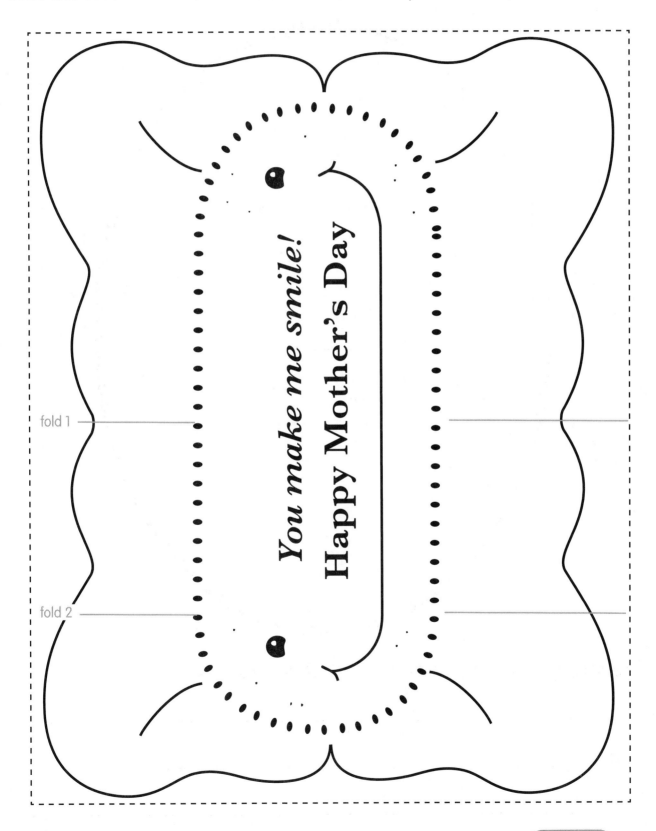

fold 1

fold 2

*You make me smile!*

**Happy Mother's Day**

Name _____

# A Surprise for Mother

Draw a line from Mother to her surprise.

What would you give your mother as a surprise on

Mother's Day?_____

Seasonal Activities • EMC 2003 • © Evan-Moor Corp.

## Calendars

## Summer Weather

## Summertime

## Father's Day

## July

Summer

Name _____

| June 🍒 | Year | Season |
|---------|------|--------|
| | _____ | winter    summer<br>spring    autumn |

Parents, please post this calendar. Help your children with the items below.

| Sunday | Monday | Tuesday | Wednesday | Thursday | Friday | Saturday |
|--------|--------|---------|-----------|----------|--------|----------|
| | | | | | | |
| | | | | | | |
| | | | | | | |
| | | | | | | |
| | | | | | | |

1. Write the number for each day in June.

2. There are always _____ days in June.

3. Draw a yellow sun on the first day of summer.

4. There are _____ Sundays in June.

5. Draw a butterfly on Father's Day.

6. Record class birthdays on your calendar.

Seasonal Activities • EMC 2003 • © Evan-Moor Corp.

Name _____

| July | | Year | Season |
|------|--|------|--------|
| | | _____ | winter    summer<br>spring    autumn |

Parents, please post this calendar. Help your children with the items below.

| Sunday | Monday | Tuesday | Wednesday | Thursday | Friday | Saturday |
|--------|--------|---------|-----------|----------|--------|----------|
| | | | | | | |
| | | | | | | |
| | | | | | | |
| | | | | | | |
| | | | | | | |

1. Write the number for each day in July.

2. There are always _____ days in July.

3. Draw a firecracker on Independence Day.

4. Which day of the week is the Fourth of July? _____

5. How many Sundays are in July? _____

6. Record class birthdays on your calendar.

Name _____

| August  | Year _____ | Season<br>winter    summer<br>spring    autumn |

Parents, please post this calendar. Help your children with the items below.

| Sunday | Monday | Tuesday | Wednesday | Thursday | Friday | Saturday |
|--------|--------|---------|-----------|----------|--------|----------|
|        |        |         |           |          |        |          |
|        |        |         |           |          |        |          |
|        |        |         |           |          |        |          |
|        |        |         |           |          |        |          |
|        |        |         |           |          |        |          |

1. Write the number for each day in August.

2. There are always _____ days in August.

3. Color every Thursday orange.

4. What day of the week is August 25? _____

5. Circle the date for each Monday in August.

6. Record class birthdays on your calendar.

Seasonal Activities • EMC 2003 • © Evan-Moor Corp.

Name _____

# Summer

Color the picture.

Fill in the blanks.

_____ is the first day of summer.
date

The weather is _____ .

Name _____

# It's Sunny!

**I**t's sunny! It's sunny!
Let's go out to play.
Put on sandals.
Grab your hat.
We'll have fun today!

Color the picture. Answer the question.

What would you do on a sunny day? _____

_____

_____

Seasonal Activities • EMC 2003 • © Evan-Moor Corp.

Name _____

# A Sunny Day

Connect the dots to see what I am going to wear on a sunny day.

Start at **A**.

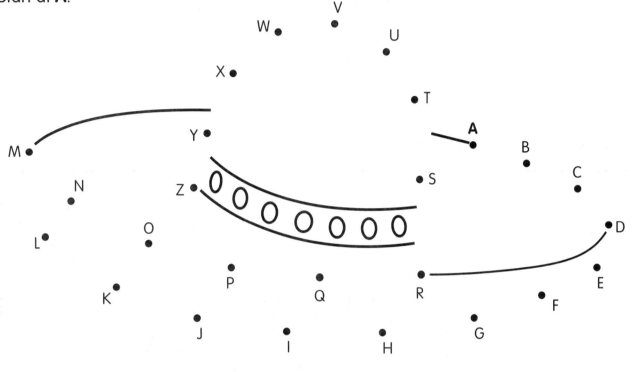

---

Start at **a**.

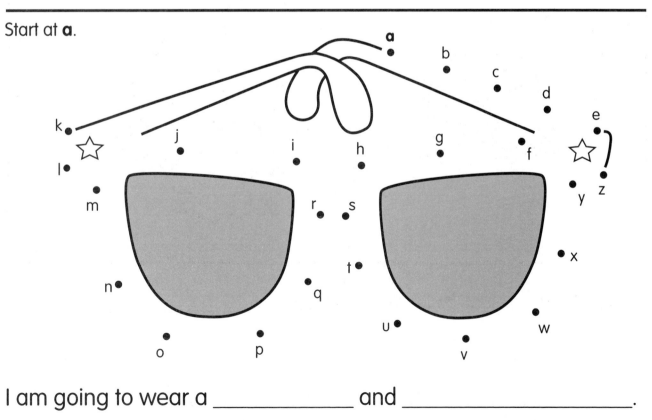

I am going to wear a _____ and _____.

# A Day at the Beach

Glue the puzzle here.

| | | |
|---|---|---|
| glue | glue | glue |
| glue | glue | glue |
| glue | glue | glue |

What do you like to do at the beach? _____

_____

_____

Seasonal Activities • EMC 2003 • © Evan-Moor Corp.

**Note:** Reproduce this puzzle to use with page 128.

Color, then cut apart the pieces.
Glue to make a picture on page 128.

Name _____

# Summer Crossword Puzzle

Read the clues.
Write the words in the boxes.
Read down the middle to find the mystery words.

**Across**

1. the month after May

2. a cool summer drink

3. you and I

4. to take a trip

5. a water animal with fins

6. light from the sun

7. a short sleep

**Word Box**

fish
June
lemonade
nap
sunshine
travel
we

Seasonal Activities • EMC 2003 • © Evan-Moor Corp.

Name _____

# Summer Fun

Circle the things that are fun to do in the summertime.

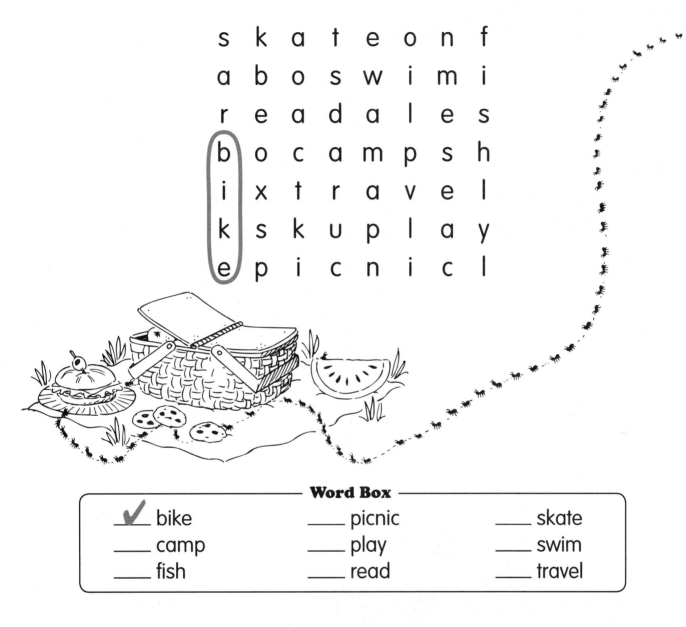

```
s  k  a  t  e  o  n  f
a  b  o  s  w  i  m  i
r  e  a  d  a  l  e  s
b  o  c  a  m  p  s  h
i  x  t  r  a  v  e  l
k  s  k  u  p  l  a  y
e  p  i  c  n  i  c  l
```

**Word Box**

| ✓ bike | ___ picnic | ___ skate |
|---|---|---|
| ___ camp | ___ play | ___ swim |
| ___ fish | ___ read | ___ travel |

What do you like to do best for summer fun?_____

_____

_____

_____

# How to Stay Cool in the Summertime

List three ways you stay cool on a hot day.

1. _____

2. _____

3. _____

Now draw one of the ways on your list.

 Seasonal Activities • EMC 2003 • © Evan-Moor Corp.

Name _____

# Back to Camp

Help the tired camper find his way back to camp.
Start at **0**. Count by **5s** to move through the maze.

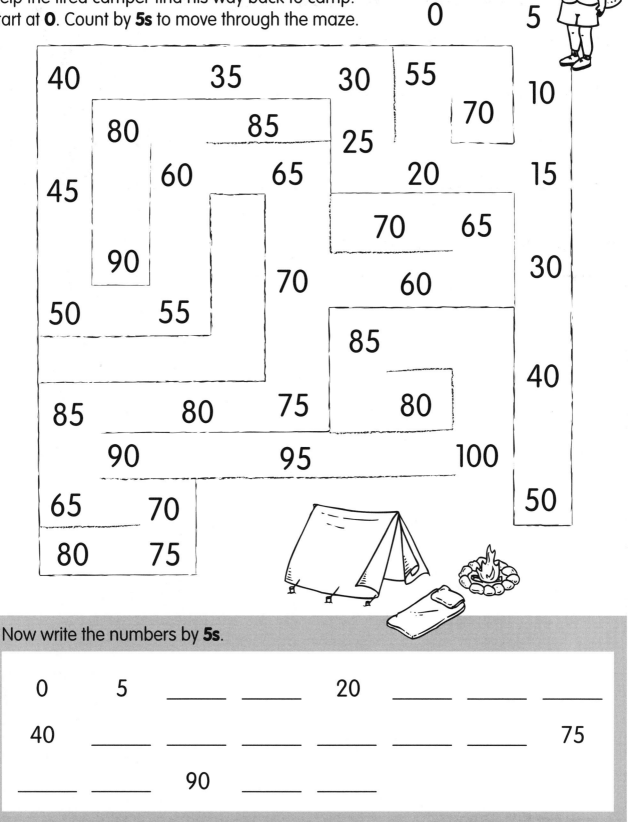

0    5

40    35    30    55    10

80    85    25    70

45    60    65    20    15

90    70    65

50    55    70    30

85    60

85

75    80    40

85    80    90    95    100

65    70    50

80    75

Now write the numbers by **5s**.

0    5    ____    ____    20    ____    ____    ____

40    ____    ____    ____    ____    ____    ____    75

____    ____    90    ____    ____    ____

# Camping Surprise

Start at **2**. Count by **2s** to find where the bear found his treat.

What did the bear find to eat? _____

Seasonal Activities • EMC 2003 • © Evan-Moor Corp.

Name _____

# My Vacation

Write about where you would like to go on vacation.

| Where will you go? | Why will you go there? |
| --- | --- |
| _____ | _____ |
| _____ | _____ |

How will you get there?

_____

_____

_____

What will you do?

_____

_____

_____

_____

_____

_____

_____

Name _____

# Fun in the Sun

Draw the other side of the picture. Draw yourself playing on the beach.
Color the picture.

Why would you need an umbrella on a sunny day?

_____

_____

# Summer Action

Read the sentences. Fill in the missing words.

> Today I **ride** my bike.
> Yesterday I **rode** my bike.

1. We **ride** in the car to the store.

   Yesterday we _____ rode _____ in the car.

2. I like to **swim** in the pool.

   Yesterday I _____ in the pool.

3. I like to **draw** with colored pencils.

   Yesterday I _____ a picture.

4. I like to **fish** in our boat.

   Yesterday I _____ in the lake.

5. I can **fly** a toy plane.

   Yesterday I _____ my toy plane.

6. I can **throw** a baseball across the yard.

   Yesterday I _____ my ball out of
   the yard.

---

**Word Box**

____ drew      ✔ rode      ____ fished
____ swam      ____ flew     ____ threw

---

# A Picnic in the Park

Draw a line to help the boy get to the picnic table.

Circle the things you eat at a picnic.

s a n d w i c h c
j p i c k l e x h
u c h i c k e n i
i y x t m i l k p
c d f r u i t m s
e z a p p l e c x

**Word Box**

____ apple

____ chicken

____ chips

____ fruit

____ juice

____ milk

____ pickle

____ sandwich

Name _____

# In the Picnic Basket

Unscramble the words. Write the name of each food in the boxes.

urtif

ociesko

lpkiec

tapoot iphsc

cuiej

hsnidawc

What would you pack in your picnic basket?

_____  _____  _____

Name _____

# What Did Matt Catch?

Subtract. Color the triangles below with the correct color and you'll see the answer.

**5**=blue    **6**=yellow    **7**=orange

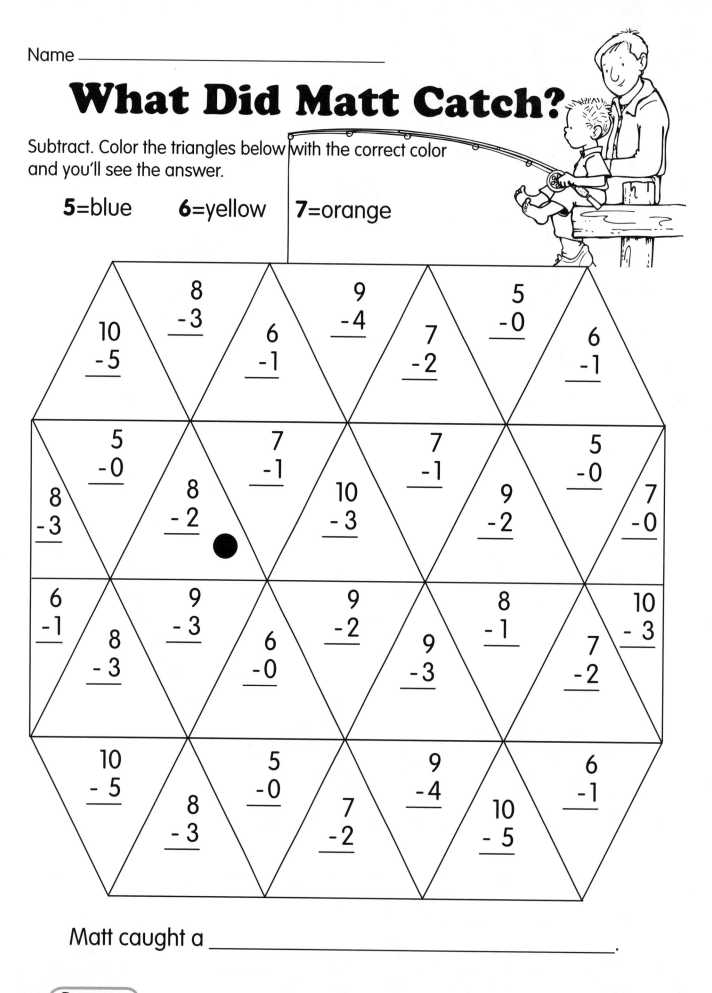

Matt caught a _____ .

Name _____

# About My Father

Draw a picture of your father. Then write about him.

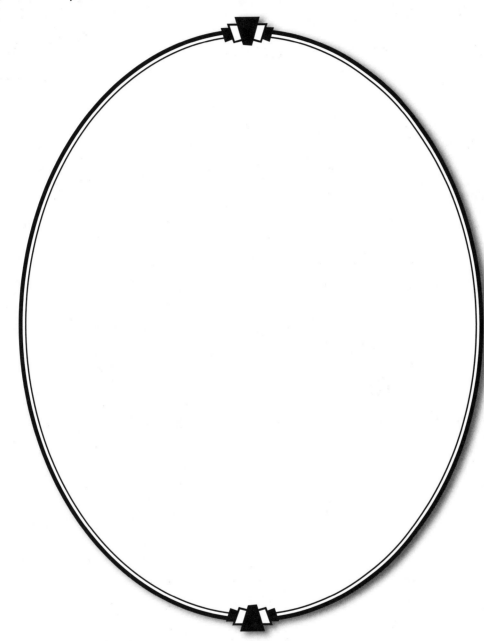

The three best things about my father are:

1. _____

2. _____

3. _____

# Happy Father's Day

Color and cut out the card. Fold on the lines. Give it to your father.

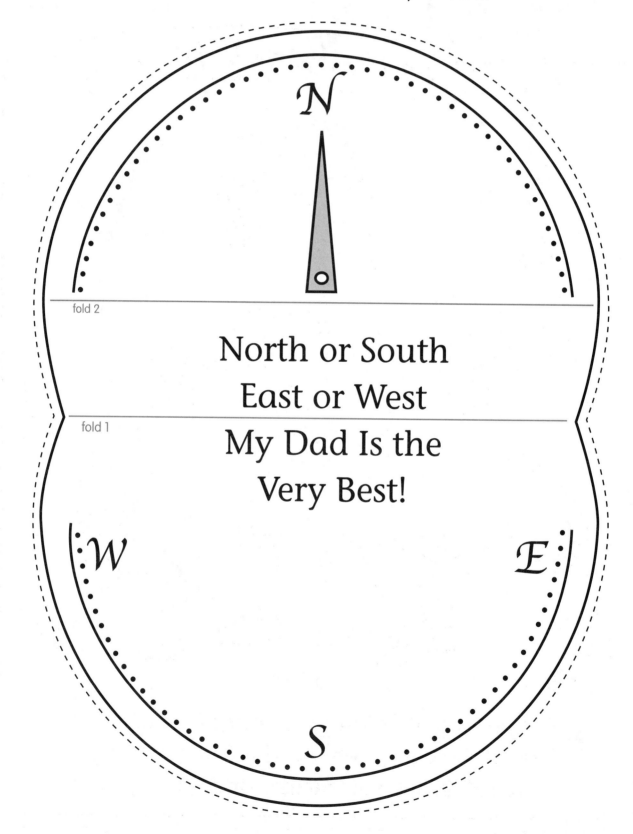

North or South
East or West

My Dad Is the
Very Best!

Seasonal Activities • EMC 2003 • © Evan-Moor Corp.

Name _____

# Fourth of July

Color the picture.

The United States of America has a birthday every year on the Fourth of July. We celebrate with picnics and fireworks.

Name _____

# The American Flag

Color the flags.

**America's first flag had:**

 7 red stripes

 6 white stripes

 13 stars

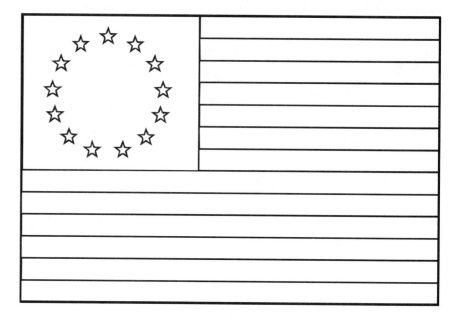

**Today, America's flag has:**

 7 red stripes

 6 white stripes

 50 stars

How are the two flags different? _____

_____

_____

_____

Name _____

# Pledge to the Flag

Read the Pledge of Allegiance, then copy it on the lines below.

> I pledge allegiance to the flag of the United States of America, and to the republic for which it stands, one nation under God, indivisible, with liberty and justice for all.

I pledge _____

_____

_____

_____

_____

_____

_____

# Answer Key

## Page 2

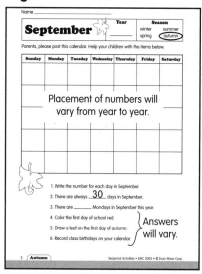

**September** | Year | Season: winter, spring, summer, autumn

Parents, please post this calendar. Help your children with the items below.

| Sunday | Monday | Tuesday | Wednesday | Thursday | Friday | Saturday |
|---|---|---|---|---|---|---|

Placement of numbers will vary from year to year.

1. Write the number for each day in September.
2. There are always **30** days in September.
3. There are _____ Mondays in September this year.
4. Color the first day of school red.
5. Draw a leaf on the first day of autumn.
6. Record class birthdays on your calendar.

Answers will vary.

Seasonal Activities • EMC 2003 • © Evan-Moor Corp.    Autumn    2

## Page 3

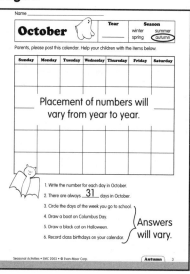

**October** | Year | Season: winter, spring, summer, autumn

Parents, please post this calendar. Help your children with the items below.

| Sunday | Monday | Tuesday | Wednesday | Thursday | Friday | Saturday |
|---|---|---|---|---|---|---|

Placement of numbers will vary from year to year.

1. Write the number for each day in October.
2. There are always **31** days in October.
3. Circle the days of the week you go to school.
4. Draw a boat on Columbus Day.
5. Draw a black cat on Halloween.
6. Record class birthdays on your calendar.

Answers will vary.

Seasonal Activities • EMC 2003 • © Evan-Moor Corp.    Autumn    3

## Page 4

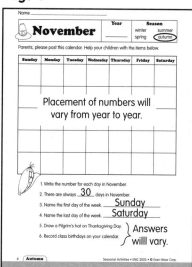

**November** | Year | Season: winter, spring, summer, autumn

Parents, please post this calendar. Help your children with the items below.

| Sunday | Monday | Tuesday | Wednesday | Thursday | Friday | Saturday |
|---|---|---|---|---|---|---|

Placement of numbers will vary from year to year.

1. Write the number for each day in November.
2. There are always **30** days in November.
3. Name the first day of the week. **Sunday**
4. Name the last day of the week. **Saturday**
5. Draw a Pilgrim's hat on Thanksgiving Day.
6. Record class birthdays on your calendar.

Answers willl vary.

Seasonal Activities • EMC 2003 • © Evan-Moor Corp.    Autumn    4

## Page 5

### Back to School

Color the tools you use at school. Check them off the list below.

_____ book    _____ crayon    _____ scissors
_____ pencil    _____ ruler    _____ paintbrush

What else is hiding in this picture?
**peanut, ball, spoon, butterfly, caterpillar**

Seasonal Activities • EMC 2003 • © Evan-Moor Corp.    Autumn    5

## Page 6

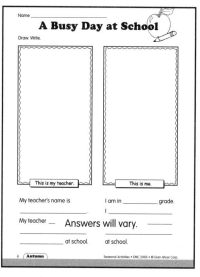

### A Busy Day at School

Draw. Write.

This is my teacher.    This is me.

My teacher's name is _____    I am in _____ grade.
I _____

My teacher **Answers will vary.**

_____ at school.    _____ at school.

6    Autumn    Seasonal Activities • EMC 2003 • © Evan-Moor Corp.

## Page 7

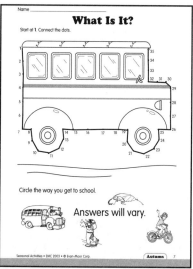

### What Is It?

Start at 1. Connect the dots.

Circle the way you get to school.

**Answers will vary.**

Seasonal Activities • EMC 2003 • © Evan-Moor Corp.    Autumn    7

## Page 8

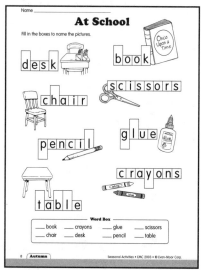

### At School

Fill in the boxes to name the pictures.

desk    book
scissors
chair
pencil    glue
crayons
table

**Word Box**
_____ book    _____ crayons    _____ glue    _____ scissors
_____ chair    _____ desk    _____ pencil    _____ table

8    Autumn    Seasonal Activities • EMC 2003 • © Evan-Moor Corp.

## Page 9

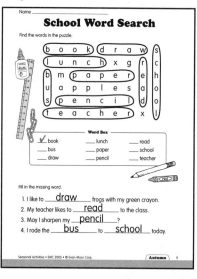

### School Word Search

Find the words in the puzzle.

b o o k d r a w s
l u n c h x g r c
b m p a p e r e h
u a p p l e s a o
s p e n c i l d o
t e a c h e r x l

**Word Box**
✓ book    _____ lunch    _____ read
_____ bus    _____ paper    _____ school
_____ draw    _____ pencil    _____ teacher

Fill in the missing word.

1. I like to **draw** frogs with my green crayon.
2. My teacher likes to **read** to the class.
3. May I sharpen my **pencil** ?
4. I rode the **bus** to **school** today.

Seasonal Activities • EMC 2003 • © Evan-Moor Corp.    Autumn    9

## Page 10

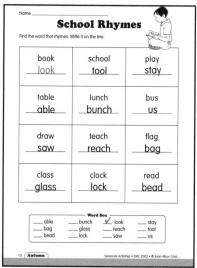

### School Rhymes

Find the word that rhymes. Write it on the line.

| book **look** | school **tool** | play **stay** |
|---|---|---|
| table **able** | lunch **bunch** | bus **us** |
| draw **saw** | teach **reach** | flag **bag** |
| class **glass** | clock **lock** | read **bead** |

**Word Box**
_____ able    _____ bunch    ✓ look    _____ stay
_____ bag    _____ glass    _____ reach    _____ tool
_____ bead    _____ lock    _____ saw    _____ us

10    Autumn    Seasonal Activities • EMC 2003 • © Evan-Moor Corp.

146    Seasonal Activities • EMC 2003 • © Evan-Moor Corp.

## Page 11

Name _____

### Autumn Weather

Color the picture.

Fill in the blanks.

September 22 is the first day of autumn.

The weather is Answers will vary.

Seasonal Activities • EMC 2003 • © Evan-Moor Corp. | Autumn | 11

## Page 12

Name _____

### Acorn Hunt

Cut out the puzzle. Glue the pieces in order in the frame.
Circle the acorns.

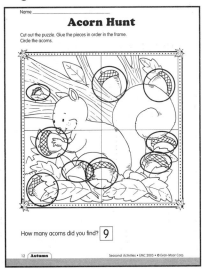

How many acorns did you find? 9

12 | Autumn | Seasonal Activities • EMC 2003 • © Evan-Moor Corp.

## Page 15

Name _____

### Falling Leaves

Find the words.
Circle them.

**Word Box**
- ✓ brown
- ___ red
- ___ fall
- ___ tree
- ___ leaf
- ___ windy
- ___ orange
- ___ yellow

Write a sentence about autumn leaves.
Answers will vary.

Seasonal Activities • EMC 2003 • © Evan-Moor Corp. | Autumn | 15

## Page 16

Name _____

### Gathering Nuts

In the autumn, squirrels are very busy.
They must find food to save for winter.

How many nuts has the squirrel picked up? Add the nuts together to see.

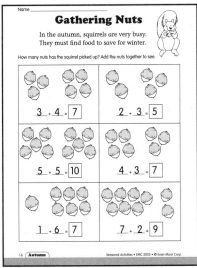

3 + 4 = 7

2 + 3 = 5

5 + 5 = 10

4 + 3 = 7

1 + 6 = 7

7 + 2 = 9

16 | Autumn | Seasonal Activities • EMC 2003 • © Evan-Moor Corp.

## Page 17

Name _____

### What Goes Together?

Find the words that
go together.
Write them on the lines.

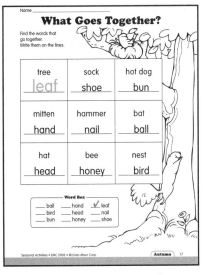

| tree | sock | hot dog |
|------|------|---------|
| leaf | shoe | bun |
| mitten | hammer | bat |
| hand | nail | ball |
| hat | bee | nest |
| head | honey | bird |

**Word Box**
- ___ ball
- ___ hand
- ✓ leaf
- ___ bird
- ___ head
- ___ nail
- ___ bun
- ___ honey
- ___ shoe

Seasonal Activities • EMC 2003 • © Evan-Moor Corp. | Autumn | 17

## Page 18

Name _____

### Autumn Crossword Puzzle

Fill in the boxes.

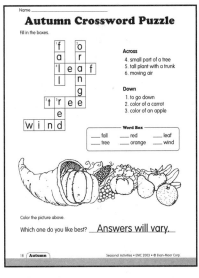

**Across**
4. small part of a tree
5. tall plant with a trunk
6. moving air

**Down**
1. to go down
2. color of a carrot
3. color of an apple

**Word Box**
- ___ fall
- ___ red
- ___ leaf
- ___ tree
- ___ orange
- ___ wind

Color the picture above.

Which one do you like best? Answers will vary.

18 | Autumn | Seasonal Activities • EMC 2003 • © Evan-Moor Corp.

## Page 20

Name _____

### Across the Ocean

Help Columbus find America
by coloring the numbers used
to count by **2s.**

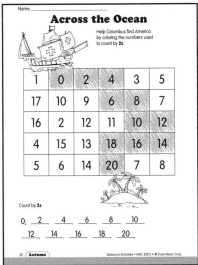

| 1 | 0 | 2 | 4 | 3 | 5 |
|---|---|---|---|---|---|
| 17 | 10 | 9 | 6 | 8 | 7 |
| 16 | 2 | 12 | 11 | 10 | 12 |
| 4 | 15 | 13 | 18 | 16 | 14 |
| 5 | 6 | 14 | 20 | 7 | 8 |

Count by **2s.**

0, 2, 4, 6, 8, 10,
12, 14, 16, 18, 20

20 | Autumn | Seasonal Activities • EMC 2003 • © Evan-Moor Corp.

## Page 22

Name _____

### Watch the Pumpkin Grow

Color and cut out the pictures. Glue them in order.

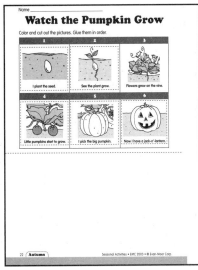

1. I plant the seed.
2. See the plant grow.
3. Flowers grow on the vine.
4. Little pumpkins start to grow.
5. I pick the big pumpkin.
6. Now I have a jack-o'-lantern.

22 | Autumn | Seasonal Activities • EMC 2003 • © Evan-Moor Corp.

## Page 23

Name _____

### Green and Orange Surprise

Start at **1**. Connect the dots.
Color the picture.

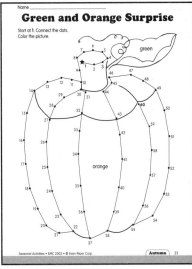

green

orange

Seasonal Activities • EMC 2003 • © Evan-Moor Corp. | Autumn | 23

## Page 24

Name _____

### Scarecrow

Draw the other side. Color the picture.

Scarecrow stands in the field all day,
waving his arms to scare birds away.

24 | Autumn     Seasonal Activities • EMC 2003 • © Evan-Moor Corp.

## Page 25

Name _____

### Halloween Word Search

Find the words.

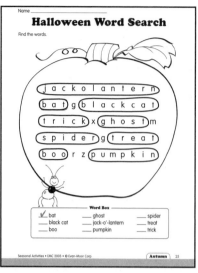

**Word Box**

| ✓ bat | ___ ghost | ___ spider |
|---|---|---|
| ___ black cat | ___ jack-o'-lantern | ___ treat |
| ___ boo | ___ pumpkin | ___ trick |

Seasonal Activities • EMC 2003 • © Evan-Moor Corp.    Autumn | 25

## Page 26

Name _____

### Mystery Words

Unscramble the words.
Draw lines to match the words to the pictures.

1. tab   b a t
2. wol   o w l
3. hstgo   g h o s t
4. thiwc   w i t c h
5. munpipk   p u m p k i n
6. bklca atc   b l a c k c a t

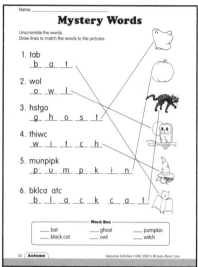

**Word Box**

| ___ bat | ___ ghost | ___ pumpkin |
|---|---|---|
| ___ black cat | ___ owl | ___ witch |

26 | Autumn     Seasonal Activities • EMC 2003 • © Evan-Moor Corp.

## Page 27

Name _____

### A Black Cat

Follow the directions to draw a cat.

Color the cat black. Add a big yellow moon.

Seasonal Activities • EMC 2003 • © Evan-Moor Corp.    Autumn | 27

## Page 29

Name _____

### The Mayflower

Start at 1. Connect the dots.

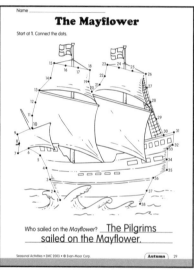

Who sailed on the *Mayflower*?   The Pilgrims sailed on the Mayflower.

Seasonal Activities • EMC 2003 • © Evan-Moor Corp.    29

## Page 33

Name _____

### Planting Corn

Plant a fish with the corn seeds.

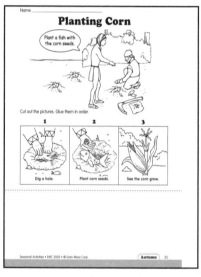

Cut out the pictures. Glue them in order.

| 1 | 2 | 3 |
|---|---|---|
| Dig a hole. | Plant corn seeds. | See the corn grow. |

Seasonal Activities • EMC 2003 • © Evan-Moor Corp.    Autumn | 33

## Page 34

Name _____

### Pilgrim Children

Underlined answers may vary.

Color the picture. Make a red X in front of what a Pilgrim child would do.
Draw a blue line under what a child today would do.

| X go to school | X go to church on Sunday |
|---|---|
| ___ watch TV | ___ eat pizza |
| X play with friends | ___ ride a bus to school |
| X help mother do housework | X dress like their parents |
| X help father hunt | ___ shop at the mall |

34 | Autumn     Seasonal Activities • EMC 2003 • © Evan-Moor Corp.

## Page 35

Name _____

### New Foods in America

The Pilgrims learned many things in America.
They learned how to hunt animals for food.
They learned how to plant new kinds of food.

Circle the foods the Pilgrims found in America.

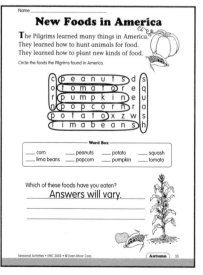

**Word Box**

| ___ corn | ___ peanuts | ___ potato | ___ squash |
|---|---|---|---|
| ___ lima beans | ___ popcorn | ___ pumpkin | ___ tomato |

Which of these foods have you eaten?
Answers will vary.

Seasonal Activities • EMC 2003 • © Evan-Moor Corp.    Autumn | 35

## Page 36

Name _____

### Wild Turkey

Draw the other side. Color the picture.

Long ago, turkeys were found only in America.
Early settlers hunted them for food.
Now turkeys are grown on farms.
We buy our turkey at the market.

36 | Autumn     Seasonal Activities • EMC 2003 • © Evan-Moor Corp.

**Page 37**

Name _____

## I Am Thankful

For sunshine and shade.
For games I have played.
For blankets at night.
And bearhugs tight.

*Jill Norris*

Draw something you are thankful for.

[ drawing box ]

I am thankful for _____

_____

Answers will vary.

**Page 38**

Name _____

## Thanksgiving Dinner at My House

Draw what you eat for Thanksgiving dinner.

My favorite part of Thanksgiving dinner is _____

Answers will vary.

**Page 40**

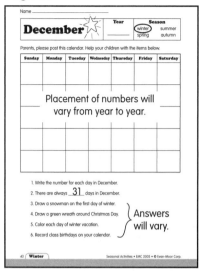

Name _____

## December ☆   Year ____   Season (winter) spring / summer autumn

Parents, please post this calendar. Help your children with the items below.

| Sunday | Monday | Tuesday | Wednesday | Thursday | Friday | Saturday |
|---|---|---|---|---|---|---|
| | | | | | | |
| | | | | | | |

Placement of numbers will vary from year to year.

1. Write the number for each day in December.
2. There are always __31__ days in December.
3. Draw a snowman on the first day of winter.
4. Draw a green wreath around Christmas Day.
5. Color each day of winter vacation.
6. Record class birthdays on your calendar.

} Answers will vary.

**Page 41**

Name _____

## January   Year ____   Season (winter) spring / summer autumn

Parents, please post this calendar. Help your children with the items below.

| Sunday | Monday | Tuesday | Wednesday | Thursday | Friday | Saturday |
|---|---|---|---|---|---|---|
| | | | | | | |
| | | | | | | |

Placement of numbers will vary from year to year.

1. Write the number for each day in January.
2. There are always __31__ days in January.
3. Make a big star on New Year's Day.
4. Outline Martin Luther King, Jr.'s birthday.
5. What day of the week is January 16?
6. Record class birthdays on your calendar.

} Answers will vary.

**Page 42**

Name _____

## February ♥   Year ____   Season (winter) spring / summer autumn

Parents, please post this calendar. Help your children with the items below.

| Sunday | Monday | Tuesday | Wednesday | Thursday | Friday | Saturday |
|---|---|---|---|---|---|---|
| | | | | | | |
| | | | | | | |

Placement of numbers will vary from year to year.

1. Write the number for each day in February.
2. There are usually __28__ days in February.
   In leap years there are __29__ days.
3. Color Groundhog Day black like a shadow.
4. Draw a red heart on Valentine's Day.
5. Circle the birthdays of George Washington and Abraham Lincoln.
6. Record class birthdays on your calendar.

Answers will vary.

**Page 43**

Name _____

## Winter

Color the picture.

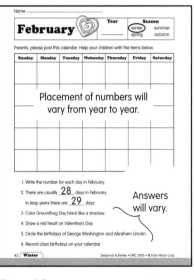

Fill in the blanks.

__December 21__ is the first day of winter.
*date*

The weather is __Answers will vary.__

**Page 44**

Name _____

## Snowflakes

Draw lines to match the snowflakes that are alike.

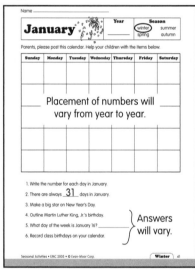

Answers will vary.

Does it snow where you live?   yes   no

**Page 45**

Name _____

## Snowy Day

Color the picture. Answer the question.

It's snowing! It's snowing!
Let's go out to play.
Put on mittens.
Grab your scarf.
We'll have fun today!

What would you do on a snowy day?

_____

Answers will vary.

**Page 46**

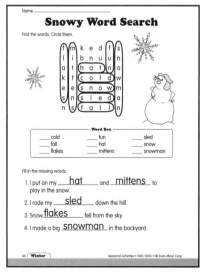

Name _____

## Snowy Word Search

Find the words. Circle them.

**Word Box**

| | | |
|---|---|---|
| ___ cold | ___ fun | ___ sled |
| ___ fall | ___ hat | ___ snow |
| ___ flakes | ___ mittens | ___ snowman |

Fill in the missing words.

1. I put on my __hat__ and __mittens__ to play in the snow.
2. I rode my __sled__ down the hill.
3. Snow__flakes__ fell from the sky.
4. I made a big __snowman__ in the backyard.

**Page 47**

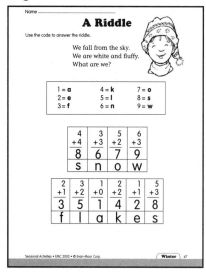

## A Riddle

Use the code to answer the riddle.

We fall from the sky.
We are white and fluffy.
What are we?

| 1 = **a** | 4 = **k** | 7 = **o** |
|---|---|---|
| 2 = **e** | 5 = **l** | 8 = **s** |
| 3 = **f** | 6 = **n** | 9 = **w** |

| 4 | 3 | 5 | 6 |
|---|---|---|---|
| +4 | +3 | +2 | +3 |
| 8 | 6 | 7 | 9 |
| s | n | o | w |

| 2 | 3 | 1 | 2 | 1 | 5 |
|---|---|---|---|---|---|
| +1 | +2 | +0 | +2 | +1 | +3 |
| 3 | 5 | 1 | 4 | 2 | 8 |
| f | l | a | k | e | s |

Seasonal Activities • EMC 2003 • © Evan-Moor Corp.   Winter 47

---

**Page 48**

## Winter Words

Write the name of each picture.

1. scarf
2. boots
3. snowman
4. sled
5. mittens
6. snowsuit
7. snowflake
8. hat
9. earmuffs

**Word Box**

___ boots   ___ mittens   ___ snowflake
___ earmuffs ___ scarf    ___ snowman
___ hat     ___ sled      ___ snowsuit

48 Winter   Seasonal Activities • EMC 2003 • © Evan-Moor Corp.

---

**Page 49**

## My Snowman

Draw the other side of the snowman. Color the picture.

Unscramble the words to make a sentence. Draw what it says about the snowman.

| nose. | My | has | carrot | snowman | a | chubby |
|---|---|---|---|---|---|---|

My snowman has a
chubby carrot nose.

Seasonal Activities • EMC 2003 • © Evan-Moor Corp.   Winter 49

---

**Page 50**

## Snow Words

Write the missing part of the word to name the picture.

snow mobile   snow ball   snow suit
snow flake    snow shoe   snow man

**Word Box**

___ ball   ___ man     ___ shoe
___ flake  ___ mobile  ___ suit

Fill in the missing word in the sentence.

1. I rode a snowmobile with my dad.
2. Did the snowman have a carrot nose?
3. Can you hit the pole with a snowball ?

50 Winter   Seasonal Activities • EMC 2003 • © Evan-Moor Corp.

---

**Page 53**

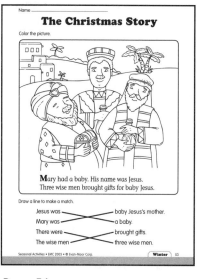

## The Christmas Story

Color the picture.

**M**ary had a baby. His name was Jesus.
Three wise men brought gifts for baby Jesus.

Draw a line to make a match.

Jesus was — baby Jesus's mother.
Mary was — a baby.
There were — brought gifts.
The wise men — three wise men.

Seasonal Activities • EMC 2003 • © Evan-Moor Corp.   Winter 53

---

**Page 54**

## A Family Celebration

Color the pictures. Answer the question.

On Christmas morning, we go to church.
After church, my family unwraps our presents.

Does your family have a Christmas celebration?   yes   no
**Answers will vary.**

54 Winter   Seasonal Activities • EMC 2003 • © Evan-Moor Corp.

---

**Page 55**

## Three Wise Men

The Three Wise Men are looking for baby Jesus.
Draw a line to help them find their way.

Seasonal Activities • EMC 2003 • © Evan-Moor Corp.   Winter 55

---

**Page 56**

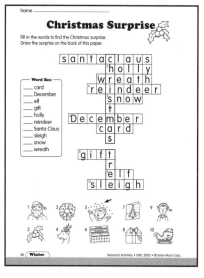

## Christmas Surprise

Fill in the words to find the Christmas surprise.
Draw the surprise on the back of this paper.

s a n t a c l a u s
holly
wreath
reindeer
snow
t
December
card
s

gift
r
elf
sleigh

**Word Box**

___ card
___ December
___ elf
___ gift
___ holly
___ reindeer
___ Santa Claus
___ sleigh
___ snow
___ wreath

56 Winter   Seasonal Activities • EMC 2003 • © Evan-Moor Corp.

---

**Page 57**

## Santa's Reindeer

Look who is ready to pull Santa's sleigh.
Follow the steps to draw one of Santa's reindeer. Color the picture.

What is the reindeer's name? **Answers will vary.**

Seasonal Activities • EMC 2003 • © Evan-Moor Corp.   Winter 57

---

## Page 58

**More Than One**

Write the word that names more than one of each thing.

**Word Box**
___ boxes
___ children
___ deer
___ feet
___ geese
___ gifts
___ men
___ mice
___ sleighs
___ teeth

man — **men**
gift — **gifts**
box — **boxes**
deer — **deer**
mouse — **mice**
tooth — **teeth**
goose — **geese**
sleigh — **sleighs**
child — **children**
foot — **feet**

58 Winter

## Page 59

**Reindeer and Elves**

Use the reindeer and elf to help you find the answers. Draw the answer to each question. Then count and write the answer.

1. How many legs do two reindeer and one elf have in all? **10** legs

2. How many tails do three reindeer and two elves have in all? **3** tails

3. How many ears do three elves and two reindeer have in all? **10** ears

Winter 59

## Page 60

**What Is It?**

Start at 1. Connect the dots. Color the picture.

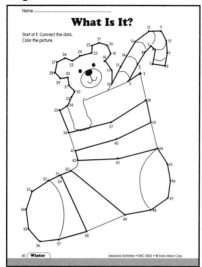

60 Winter

## Page 61

**Riddle Time**

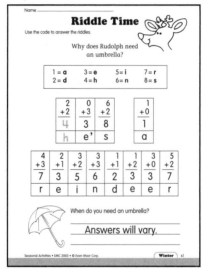

Use the code to answer the riddles.

Why does Rudolph need an umbrella?

| 1 = a | 3 = e | 5 = i | 7 = r |
| 2 = d | 4 = h | 6 = n | 8 = s |

| 2 +2 = 4 | 0 +3 = 3 | 6 +2 = 8 | | 1 +0 = 1 |
| h | e' | s | | a |

| 4 +3 = 7 | 2 +1 = 3 | 3 +2 = 5 | 3 +3 = 6 | 1 +1 = 2 | 1 +2 = 3 | 3 +0 = 3 | 5 +2 = 7 |
| r | e | i | n | d | e | e | r |

When do you need an umbrella?
**Answers will vary.**

Winter 61

## Page 62

**Hanukkah**

Read the story. Color the picture.

Jewish families get together each night of Hanukkah. They light the menorah. It holds the candles they light each night. Two candles are lit the first night. One more candle is lit each night. On the eighth night, all of the candles are lit.

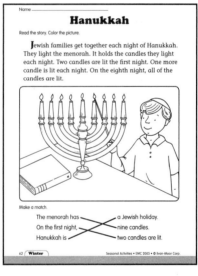

Make a match.

The menorah has — a Jewish holiday.
On the first night, — nine candles.
Hanukkah is — two candles are lit.

62 Winter

## Page 63

**A Family Celebration**

Color the picture. Answer the questions.

My family has a special feast for Hanukkah. We play games and sing. We eat special foods. Children receive money and play with tops called dreidels.

**Answers will vary.**

Does your family celebrate Hanukkah?   yes   no
Have you ever played with a dreidel?   yes   no

Winter 63

## Page 64

**Spin, Dreidel, Spin**

Connect the dots. Start at **0** and count by **10s**. Color the picture.

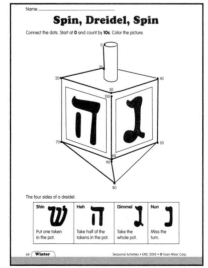

The four sides of a dreidel:

| Shin ש | Heh ה | Gimmel ג | Nun נ |
| Put one token in the pot. | Take half of the tokens in the pot. | Take the whole pot. | Miss the turn. |

64 Winter

## Page 65

**Kwanzaa**

Read the story. Color the candles red, black, and green.

Kwanzaa is an African-American holiday. Kwanzaa celebrates family history. It lasts for seven days. Each day has a special meaning to think about. A candle is lit on a kinara every day.

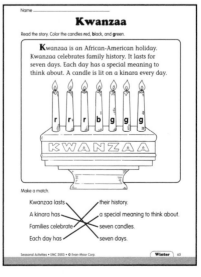

Make a match.

Kwanzaa lasts — their history.
A kinara has — a special meaning to think about.
Families celebrate — seven candles.
Each day has — seven days.

Winter 65

## Page 66

**A Family Celebration**

Color the picture. Answer the question.

My family celebrates Kwanzaa for seven days. We share stories about our family history. We eat, sing, and play music. Children get African or homemade gifts.

Does your family celebrate Kwanzaa?   yes   no
**Answers will vary.**

64 Winter

## Page 67

**A New Year**

There are twelve months in a year.

Start at **January**. Connect the dots.

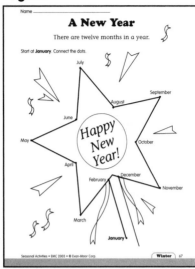

Happy New Year!

## Page 68

**The Months of the Year**

Write the name of each month in the correct order.

| January | has 31 days. |
| February | has 28 days. |
| March | has 31 days. |
| April | has 30 days. |
| May | has 31 days. |
| June | has 30 days. |
| July | has 31 days. |
| August | has 31 days. |
| September | has 30 days. |
| October | has 31 days. |
| November | has 30 days. |
| December | has 31 days. |

**Word Box**
- April
- August
- December
- February
- January
- July
- June
- March
- May
- November
- October
- September

## Page 69

**Martin Luther King, Jr., Day**

Cut out the pieces. Glue them to finish the picture.

**T**his is a day to celebrate a hero. Martin Luther King, Jr., wanted everyone to be treated fairly.
- He led marches.
- He gave speeches.
- He worked to change laws.

He helped to make the world a better place.

## Page 71

**Groundhog Day**

Read the story. Answer the questions.

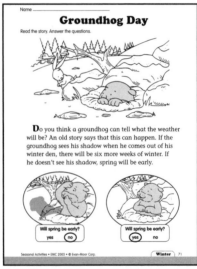

**D**o you think a groundhog can tell what the weather will be? An old story says that this can happen. If the groundhog sees his shadow when he comes out of his winter den, there will be six more weeks of winter. If he doesn't see his shadow, spring will be early.

Will spring be early? yes **no**

Will spring be early? **yes** no

## Page 72

**Groundhog's Shadow**

Draw a line to match each groundhog to its shadow.

When Groundhog sees his shadow _____
**there will be six more weeks of winter.**

## Page 75

**George Washington**

**G**eorge Washington was born on February 22 in Virginia. He became the first president of the United States of America.

Draw the other side. Color the picture.

Why do you think he is called the "Father of Our Country"?
**Answers will vary, but should include something about him being our first president.**

## Page 76

**Abraham Lincoln**

**A**braham Lincoln was born on February 12 in Kentucky. He was the 16th president of the United States of America.

Circle the numbers 1 through 16 with a red crayon.

Why do you think he was called "Honest Abe"?
**Answers will vary.**

## Page 77

**Valentine's Day**

Draw a line to match the two sides of each valentine.

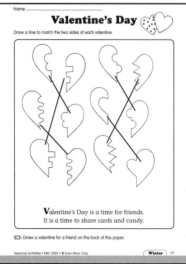

**V**alentine's Day is a time for friends. It is a time to share cards and candy.

Draw a valentine for a friend on the back of this paper.

## Page 78

**Where Are the Hearts?**

Find the hidden hearts. Color them.

How many hearts did you find? 17

**Page 79**

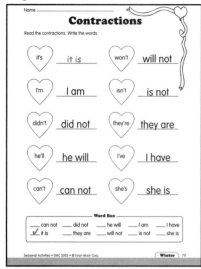

Name _____

## Contractions

Read the contractions. Write the words.

it's ___it is___    won't ___will not___

I'm ___I am___    isn't ___is not___

didn't ___did not___    they're ___they are___

he'll ___he will___    I've ___I have___

can't ___can not___    she's ___she is___

**Word Box**
___ can not  ___ did not  ___ he will  ___ I am  ___ I have
✓ it is  ___ they are  ___ will not  ___ is not  ___ she is

Seasonal Activities • EMC 2003 • © Evan-Moor Corp.    Winter  79

---

**Page 80**

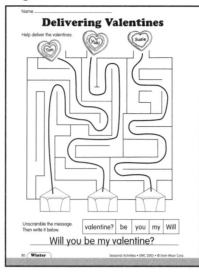

Name _____

## Delivering Valentines

Help deliver the valentines.

Tom    Yuki    Susie

Unscramble the message. Then write it below.

| valentine? | be | you | my | Will |

___Will you be my valentine?___

80  Winter    Seasonal Activities • EMC 2003 • © Evan-Moor Corp.

---

**Page 82**

Name _____

| March | | Year | Season |
| | | _____ | winter summer / spring autumn |

Parents, please post this calendar. Help your children with the items below.

| Sunday | Monday | Tuesday | Wednesday | Thursday | Friday | Saturday |
|---|---|---|---|---|---|---|
| | | | | | | |

Placement of numbers will vary from year to year.

1. Write the number for each day in March.
2. There are always ___31___ days in March.
3. Draw a flower on the first day of spring.
4. Circle each Friday in March.
5. Draw a shamrock on Saint Patrick's Day.
6. Record class birthdays on your calendar.

Answers will vary.

82  Spring    Seasonal Activities • EMC 2003 • © Evan-Moor Corp.

---

**Page 83**

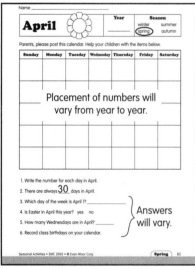

Name _____

| April | | Year | Season |
| | | _____ | winter summer / spring autumn |

Parents, please post this calendar. Help your children with the items below.

| Sunday | Monday | Tuesday | Wednesday | Thursday | Friday | Saturday |
|---|---|---|---|---|---|---|
| | | | | | | |

Placement of numbers will vary from year to year.

1. Write the number for each day in April.
2. There are always ___30___ days in April.
3. Which day of the week is April 1? _____
4. Is Easter in April this year?  yes  no
5. How many Wednesdays are in April? _____
6. Record class birthdays on your calendar.

Answers will vary.

Seasonal Activities • EMC 2003 • © Evan-Moor Corp.    Spring  83

---

**Page 84**

Name _____

| May | | Year | Season |
| | | _____ | winter summer / spring autumn |

Parents, please post this calendar. Help your children with the items below.

| Sunday | Monday | Tuesday | Wednesday | Thursday | Friday | Saturday |
|---|---|---|---|---|---|---|
| | | | | | | |

Placement of numbers will vary from year to year.

1. Write the number for each day in May.
2. There are always ___31___ days in May.
3. Outline Mother's Day with your favorite color.
4. Draw a basket of spring flowers on May Day.
5. How many Sundays are there in May? _____
6. Record class birthdays on your calendar.

Answers will vary.

84  Spring    Seasonal Activities • EMC 2003 • © Evan-Moor Corp.

---

**Page 85**

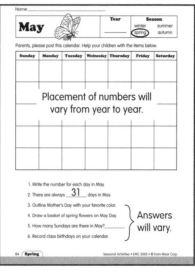

Name _____

## Spring

Color the picture.

Fill in the blanks.

___March 20___ is the first day of spring.
date

The weather is ___Answers will vary.___

Seasonal Activities • EMC 2003 • © Evan-Moor Corp.    Spring  85

---

**Page 86**

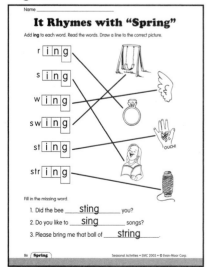

Name _____

## It Rhymes with "Spring"

Add **ing** to each word. Read the words. Draw a line to the correct picture.

r [i][n][g]
s [i][n][g]
w [i][n][g]
sw [i][n][g]
st [i][n][g]
str [i][n][g]

Fill in the missing word.

1. Did the bee ___sting___ you?
2. Do you like to ___sing___ songs?
3. Please bring me that ball of ___string___

86  Spring    Seasonal Activities • EMC 2003 • © Evan-Moor Corp.

---

**Page 87**

Name _____

## A Windy Day

Color the picture. Answer the question.

Wind's blowing! Wind's blowing!
Let's go out to play.
Put on a sweater.
Grab your kite.
We'll have fun today.

What would you do on a windy day? _____
___Answers will vary.___

Seasonal Activities • EMC 2003 • © Evan-Moor Corp.    Spring  87

---

**Page 88**

Name _____

## April Showers

Draw the other side. Add raindrops falling from the clouds. Color the picture.

Rain is water that falls from the clouds.
A cloud is made of millions of little drops of water.
When a cloud gets full of water, raindrops begin to fall.

88  Spring    Seasonal Activities • EMC 2003 • © Evan-Moor Corp.

---

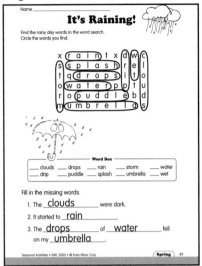

**It's Raining!**

Find the rainy day words in the word search. Circle the words you find.

x r a i n t x d w c
s s p l a s h r e l
t q d r o p s i t o
o w a t e r p p t u
r o p u d d l e b d
m u m b r e l l a s

**Word Box**
__ clouds  __ drops  __ rain  __ storm  __ water
__ drip  __ puddle  __ splash  __ umbrella  __ wet

Fill in the missing words.
1. The _clouds_ were dark.
2. It started to _rain_.
3. The _drops_ of _water_ fell on my _umbrella_.

**Rainbow**

Draw a rainbow and color it.
What colors will you use?

When rain falls down
And the sun shines behind,
You can see a rainbow,
It's easy to find!

red
orange
yellow
green
blue
purple

I see red, orange, yellow, green, blue, and purple in the rainbow.

**Dress for a Rainy Day**

Connect the dots, counting by 5s. Color the picture.

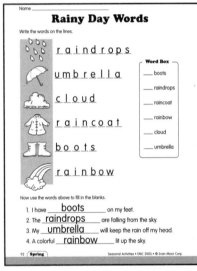

**Rainy Day Words**

Write the words on the lines.

raindrops
umbrella
cloud
raincoat
boots
rainbow

**Word Box**
__ boots
__ raindrops
__ raincoat
__ rainbow
__ cloud
__ umbrella

Now use the words above to fill in the blanks.
1. I have _boots_ on my feet.
2. The _raindrops_ are falling from the sky.
3. My _umbrella_ will keep the rain off my head.
4. A colorful _rainbow_ lit up the sky.

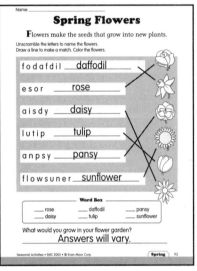

**Spring Flowers**

Flowers make the seeds that grow into new plants.

Unscramble the letters to name the flowers.
Draw a line to make a match. Color the flowers.

fodafdil — _daffodil_
esor — _rose_
aisdy — _daisy_
lutip — _tulip_
anpsy — _pansy_
flowsuner — _sunflower_

**Word Box**
__ rose  __ daffodil  __ pansy
__ daisy  __ tulip  __ sunflower

What would you grow in your flower garden?
_Answers will vary._

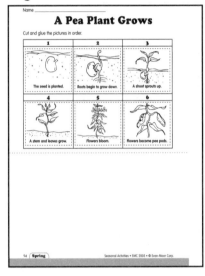

**A Pea Plant Grows**

Cut and glue the pictures in order.

1. The seed is planted.
2. Roots begin to grow down.
3. A shoot sprouts up.
4. A stem and leaves grow.
5. Flowers bloom.
6. Flowers become pea pods.

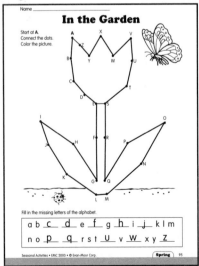

**In the Garden**

Start at A.
Connect the dots.
Color the picture.

Fill in the missing letters of the alphabet.

a b c _d_ e f g _h_ i _j_ k l m
n o _p_ q r s t _u_ v _w_ x y _z_

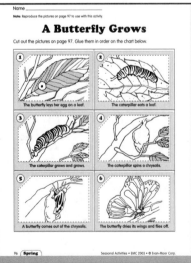

**A Butterfly Grows**

Note: Reproduce the pictures on page 97 to use with this activity.

Cut out the pictures on page 97. Glue them in order on the chart below.

1. The butterfly lays her egg on a leaf.
2. The caterpillar eats a leaf.
3. The caterpillar grows and grows.
4. The caterpillar spins a chrysalis.
5. A butterfly comes out of the chrysalis.
6. The butterfly dries its wings and flies off.

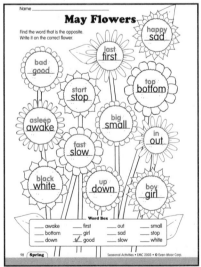

**May Flowers**

Find the word that is the opposite.
Write it on the correct flower.

happy — sad
last — first
bad — good
start — stop
top — bottom
asleep — awake
big — small
fast — slow
in — out
black — white
up — down
boy — girl

**Word Box**
__ awake  __ first  __ out  __ small
__ bottom  __ girl  __ sad  __ stop
__ down  ✓ good  __ slow  __ white

## Page 99

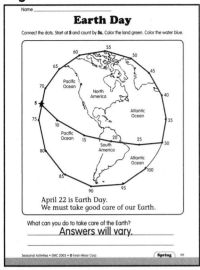

**Earth Day**

Connect the dots. Start at **5** and count by **5s**. Color the land green. Color the water blue.

April 22 is Earth Day.
We must take good care of our Earth.

What can you do to take care of the Earth?
_Answers will vary._

Seasonal Activities • EMC 2003 • © Evan-Moor Corp.  Spring  99

## Page 100

**Clean Up the Earth**

Color the picture.

Don't be a litterbug.
Pick up litter to keep the Earth clean.
Put the litter in the garbage can.

How many words can you make out of the letters in **trash**?
_Answers will vary._

100  Spring  Seasonal Activities • EMC 2003 • © Evan-Moor Corp.

## Page 102

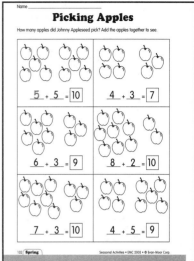

**Picking Apples**

How many apples did Johnny Appleseed pick? Add the apples together to see.

$\underline{5} + \underline{5} = \boxed{10}$     $\underline{4} + \underline{3} = \boxed{7}$

$\underline{6} + \underline{3} = \boxed{9}$     $\underline{8} + \underline{2} = \boxed{10}$

$\underline{7} + \underline{3} = \boxed{10}$     $\underline{4} + \underline{5} = \boxed{9}$

102  Spring  Seasonal Activities • EMC 2003 • © Evan-Moor Corp.

## Page 103

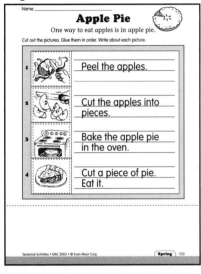

**Apple Pie**

One way to eat apples is in apple pie.

Cut out the pictures. Glue them in order. Write about each picture.

1. Peel the apples.
2. Cut the apples into pieces.
3. Bake the apple pie in the oven.
4. Cut a piece of pie. Eat it.

Seasonal Activities • EMC 2003 • © Evan-Moor Corp.  Spring  103

## Page 104

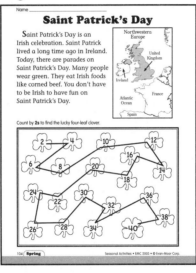

**Saint Patrick's Day**

Saint Patrick's Day is an Irish celebration. Saint Patrick lived a long time ago in Ireland. Today, there are parades on Saint Patrick's Day. Many people wear green. They eat Irish foods like corned beef. You don't have to be Irish to have fun on Saint Patrick's Day.

Count by **2s** to find the lucky four-leaf clover.

104  Spring  Seasonal Activities • EMC 2003 • © Evan-Moor Corp.

## Page 105

**Leprechaun**

Follow the steps to draw a leprechaun.

A leprechaun is a magical little person in Irish stories. Some stories say that if you catch a leprechaun, he has to give you his pot of gold.

Color the leprechaun's suit green.
Make his hair orange. Draw a pot of gold next to the leprechaun.

Seasonal Activities • EMC 2003 • © Evan-Moor Corp.  Spring  105

## Page 106

**Easter Sunday**

Start at **A**. Connect the dots.

Easter Sunday is an important day to Christians.
They go to church for special Easter services.

106  Spring  Seasonal Activities • EMC 2003 • © Evan-Moor Corp.

## Page 107

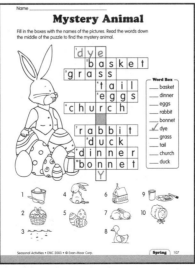

**Mystery Animal**

Fill in the boxes with the names of the pictures. Read the words down the middle of the puzzle to find the mystery animal.

d y e
b a s k e t
g r a s s
t a i l
e g g s
c h u r c h
r a b b i t
d u c k
d i n n e r
b o n n e t

**Word Box**
___ basket
___ dinner
___ eggs
___ rabbit
✓ dye
___ grass
___ tail
___ church
___ duck

107  Spring  Seasonal Activities • EMC 2003 • © Evan-Moor Corp.

## Page 108

**How to Dye an Easter Egg**

Cut out the sentences below. Glue them in order in the numbered boxes.

1. Get cups and spoons. Set them on the table.
2. Put dye in each cup. Add water and vinegar. Stir.
3. Put eggs in the cups. Turn the eggs with a spoon.
4. Lift the eggs out and let them dry.

108  Spring  Seasonal Activities • EMC 2003 • © Evan-Moor Corp.

## Page 109

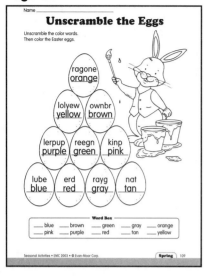

**Unscramble the Eggs**

Unscramble the color words.
Then color the Easter eggs.

ragone **orange**

lolyew **yellow**  ownbr **brown**

lerpup **purple**  reegn **green**  kinp **pink**

lube **blue**  erd **red**  rayg **gray**  nat **tan**

**Word Box**
___ blue  ___ brown  ___ green  ___ gray  ___ orange
___ pink  ___ purple  ___ red  ___ tan  ___ yellow

## Page 110

**Cheep! Cheep!**

Draw the other side of the chick and egg. Color the picture.

What is happening in the picture?
A chick is hatching out of an egg.

## Page 111

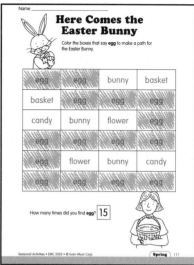

**Here Comes the Easter Bunny**

Color the boxes that say **egg** to make a path for
the Easter Bunny.

| egg | egg | bunny | basket |
| basket | egg | egg | egg |
| candy | bunny | flower | egg |
| egg | egg | egg | egg |
| egg | flower | bunny | candy |
| egg | egg | egg | egg |

How many times did you find **egg**? 15

## Page 112

**Fiesta!**

Cut out the pieces. Glue them to finish the puzzle.

People come to the fiesta
to celebrate Cinco de Mayo.

## Page 113

**Piñatas**

Color the piñatas. Answer the questions.

Piñatas first came from Mexico. They were animal
or star shapes. The piñatas were filled with tasty treats.
A piñata was hung up high. Children tried to hit the
piñata with a stick. When the piñata broke, the treats
fell to the ground. Children picked up the treats.

Now piñatas are found in many lands. They are
made in all kinds of shapes and sizes. Children still
try to break the piñata and pick up the tasty treats.

Have you ever played the piñata game?   yes   no
What tasty treats fell out of the piñata? **Answers will vary.**

## Page 114

**May Day**

Draw flowers in the basket.

Who would you surprise with a basket of flowers? Tell why.

Answers will vary.

## Page 115

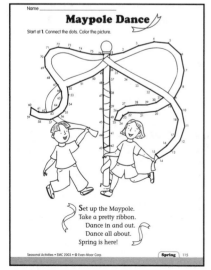

**Maypole Dance**

Start at **1**. Connect the dots. Color the picture.

Set up the Maypole.
Take a pretty ribbon.
Dance in and out.
Dance all about.
Spring is here!

## Page 118

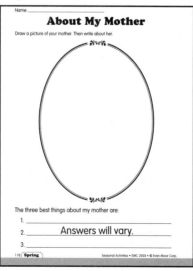

**About My Mother**

Draw a picture of your mother. Then write about her.

The three best things about my mother are:
1. _____
2. _____ Answers will vary. _____
3. _____

## Page 120

**A Surprise for Mother**

Draw a line from Mother to her surprise.

What would you give your mother as a surprise on
Mother's Day?   Answers will vary.

## Page 122

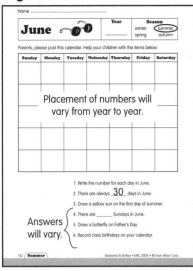

**June** — Year ____ — Season: winter, spring, **summer**, autumn

Parents, please post this calendar. Help your children with the items below.

| Sunday | Monday | Tuesday | Wednesday | Thursday | Friday | Saturday |
|--------|--------|---------|-----------|----------|--------|----------|

Placement of numbers will vary from year to year.

1. Write the number for each day in June.
2. There are always __30__ days in June.
3. Draw a yellow sun on the first day of summer.
4. There are _____ Sundays in June.
5. Draw a butterfly on Father's Day.
6. Record class birthdays on your calendar.

Answers will vary.

122 Summer — Seasonal Activities • EMC 2003 • © Evan-Moor Corp.

## Page 123

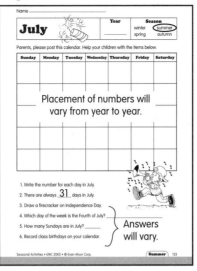

**July** — Year ____ — Season: winter, spring, **summer**, autumn

Parents, please post this calendar. Help your children with the items below.

| Sunday | Monday | Tuesday | Wednesday | Thursday | Friday | Saturday |
|--------|--------|---------|-----------|----------|--------|----------|

Placement of numbers will vary from year to year.

1. Write the number for each day in July.
2. There are always __31__ days in July.
3. Draw a firecracker on Independence Day.
4. Which day of the week is the Fourth of July?
5. How many Sundays are in July? _____
6. Record class birthdays on your calendar.

Answers will vary.

Seasonal Activities • EMC 2003 • © Evan-Moor Corp. — Summer 123

## Page 124

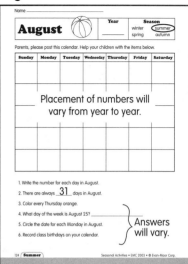

**August** — Year ____ — Season: winter, spring, **summer**, autumn

Parents, please post this calendar. Help your children with the items below.

| Sunday | Monday | Tuesday | Wednesday | Thursday | Friday | Saturday |
|--------|--------|---------|-----------|----------|--------|----------|

Placement of numbers will vary from year to year.

1. Write the number for each day in August.
2. There are always __31__ days in August.
3. Color every Thursday orange.
4. What day of the week is August 25? _____
5. Circle the date for each Monday in August.
6. Record class birthdays on your calendar.

Answers will vary.

124 Summer — Seasonal Activities • EMC 2003 • © Evan-Moor Corp.

## Page 125

### Summer

Color the picture.

Fill in the blanks.

__June 21__ is the first day of summer.

The weather is __Answers will vary.__

Seasonal Activities • EMC 2003 • © Evan-Moor Corp. — Summer 125

## Page 126

### It's Sunny!

It's sunny! It's sunny!
Let's go out to play.
Put on sandals.
Grab your hat.
We'll have fun today!

Color the picture. Answer the question.

What would you do on a sunny day? _____
__Answers will vary.__

126 Summer — Seasonal Activities • EMC 2003 • © Evan-Moor Corp.

## Page 127

### A Sunny Day

Connect the dots to see what I am going to wear on a sunny day.
Start at **A**.

Start at **a**.

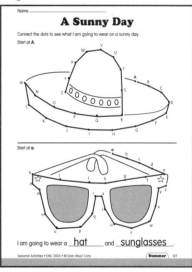

I am going to wear a __hat__ and __sunglasses__.

Seasonal Activities • EMC 2003 • © Evan-Moor Corp. — Summer 127

## Page 128

### A Day at the Beach

Glue the puzzle here.

What do you like to do at the beach?
__Answers will vary.__

128 Summer — Seasonal Activities • EMC 2003 • © Evan-Moor Corp.

## Page 130

### Summer Crossword Puzzle

Read the clues.
Write the words in the boxes.
Read down the middle to find the mystery words.

**Across**
1. the month after May
2. a cool summer drink
3. you and I
4. to take a trip
5. a water animal with fins
6. light from the sun
7. a short nap

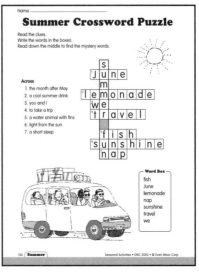

J U N E
s u m
lemonade
w e
t r a v e l
f i s h
s u n s h i n e
n a p

**Word Box**
fish
June
lemonade
nap
sunshine
travel
we

130 Summer — Seasonal Activities • EMC 2003 • © Evan-Moor Corp.

## Page 131

### Summer Fun

Circle the things that are fun to do in the summertime.

```
s k a t e o n f
a b o s w i m i
r e a d a l e s
b o c a m p s h
i x t r a v e l
k s k u p l a y
e p i c n i c l
```

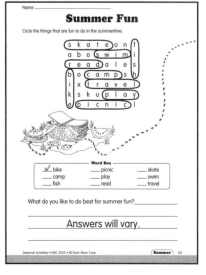

**Word Box**
- ✓ bike
- ___ camp
- ___ fish
- ___ picnic
- ___ play
- ___ read
- ___ skate
- ___ swim
- ___ travel

What do you like to do best for summer fun? _____
__Answers will vary.__

Seasonal Activities • EMC 2003 • © Evan-Moor Corp. — Summer 131

## Page 132

Name

### How to Stay Cool in the Summertime

List three ways you stay cool on a hot day.

1. _____
2. ____ Answers will vary. ____
3. _____

Now draw one of the ways on your list.

132 Summer      Seasonal Activities • EMC 2003 • © Evan-Moor Corp.

## Page 133

### Back to Camp

Help the tired camper find his way back to camp.
Start at **O**. Count by **5s** to move through the maze.

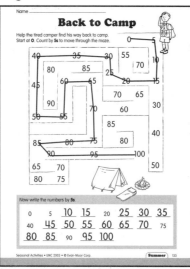

Now write the numbers by **5s**

| 0 | 5 | 10 | 15 | 20 | 25 | 30 | 35 |
|---|---|----|----|----|----|----|----|
| 40 | 45 | 50 | 55 | 60 | 65 | 70 | 75 |
| 80 | 85 | 90 | 95 | 100 | | | |

Seasonal Activities • EMC 2003 • © Evan-Moor Corp.      Summer 133

## Page 134

### Camping Surprise

Start at **2**. Count by **2s** to find where the bear found his treat.

What did the bear find to eat? _a cookie/doughnut/bagel_

134 Summer      Seasonal Activities • EMC 2003 • © Evan-Moor Corp.

## Page 135

### My Vacation

Write about where you would like to go on vacation.

| Where will you go? | Why will you go there? |
|---|---|
| | |

How will you get there?

____ Answers will vary. ____

What will you do?

Seasonal Activities • EMC 2003 • © Evan-Moor Corp.      Summer 135

## Page 136

### Fun in the Sun

Draw the other side of the picture. Draw yourself playing on the beach.
Color the picture.

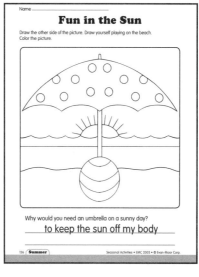

Why would you need an umbrella on a sunny day?
_to keep the sun off my body_

136 Summer      Seasonal Activities • EMC 2003 • © Evan-Moor Corp.

## Page 137

### Summer Action

Read the sentences. Fill in the missing words.

Today I **ride** my bike.
Yesterday I **rode** my bike.

1. We **ride** in the car to the store.
   Yesterday we ____ rode ____ in the car.
2. I like to **swim** in the pool.
   Yesterday I ____ swam ____ in the pool.
3. I like to **draw** with colored pencils.
   Yesterday I ____ drew ____ a picture.
4. I like to **fish** in our boat.
   Yesterday I ____ fished ____ in the lake.
5. I can **fly** a toy plane.
   Yesterday I ____ flew ____ my toy plane.
6. I can **throw** a baseball across the yard.
   Yesterday I ____ threw ____ my ball out of the yard.

**Word Box**
| ____ drew | ✓ rode | ____ fished |
|---|---|---|
| ____ swam | ____ flew | ____ threw |

Seasonal Activities • EMC 2003 • © Evan-Moor Corp.      Summer 137

## Page 138

### A Picnic in the Park

Draw a line to help the boy get to the picnic table.

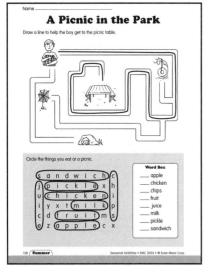

Circle the things you eat at a picnic.

s a n d w i c h c
j p i c k l e x h
u c h i c k e n i
y x t m i l k m p
d f r u i t m s
e z a p p l e c x

**Word Box**
____ apple
____ chicken
____ chips
____ fruit
____ juice
____ milk
____ pickle
____ sandwich

138 Summer      Seasonal Activities • EMC 2003 • © Evan-Moor Corp.

## Page 139

### In the Picnic Basket

Unscramble the words. Write the name of each food in the boxes.

f r u i t
urtif

c o o k i e s
ociesko

p i c k l e
lpkiec

p o t a t o c h i p s
tapoot iphsc

j u i c e
cuiej

s a n d w i c h
hsnidawc

What would you pack in your picnic basket?
_ Answers will vary. _

Seasonal Activities • EMC 2003 • © Evan-Moor Corp.      Summer 139

## Page 140

### What Did Matt Catch?

Subtract. Color the triangles below with the correct color
and you'll see the answer.

**5=blue**    **6=yellow**    **7=orange**

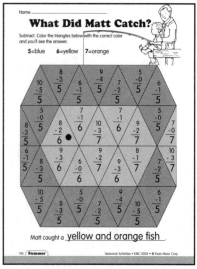

Matt caught a _yellow and orange fish_

140 Summer      Seasonal Activities • EMC 2003 • © Evan-Moor Corp.

**Page 141**

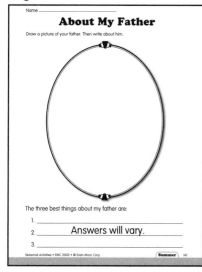

**About My Father**

Draw a picture of your father. Then write about him.

The three best things about my father are:

1. _____
2. _____ Answers will vary.
3. _____

**Page 144**

**The American Flag**

Color the flags.

**America's first flag had:**
★ 7 red stripes
★ 6 white stripes
★ 13 stars

blue

**Today, America's flag has:**
★ 7 red stripes
★ 6 white stripes
★ 50 stars

red
white
red
white

How are the two flags different? The first flag had 13 stars. Today's flag has 50 stars. **OR** They do not have the same number of stars.

**Page 145**

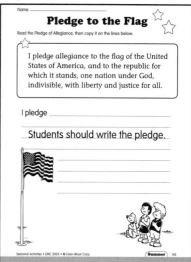

**Pledge to the Flag**

Read the Pledge of Allegiance, then copy it on the lines below.

I pledge allegiance to the flag of the United States of America, and to the republic for which it stands, one nation under God, indivisible, with liberty and justice for all.

I pledge _____

_____ Students should write the pledge. _____